A Seed
Will Meet
Any Need

A Seed Will Meet Any Need

By Keith A. Butler

Harrison House
Tulsa, Oklahoma

05 04 03 02 01   10 9 8 7 6 5 4 3 2 1

A Seed Will Meet Any Need
ISBN 1-57794-375-9
Copyright © 1998 Word of Faith Publishing
20000 W. Nine Mile Road
Southfield, MI 48075-5597

Published by Harrison House, Inc.
P.O. Box 35035
Tulsa, Oklahoma 74153

Contents

Obedience Brings the Blessing

The Bible says that God will supply all our needs by His riches in glory by Christ Jesus (Phil. 4:19.) Well, why then are so many Christians living in lack? If God wants His children to prosper, why are so many of them living in poverty?

I want to share with you a way to have all your needs met — not in heaven, but here, *now*, in this life. You need to understand that you have a part to play in your prosperity. You can't live any way you want or do anything you feel like doing and expect God to pour out a blessing on you.

There are three things that God requires of you so that He can meet any need you will ever have: *obedience, faith,* and *seed.* Once you have faithfully done your part by obeying God, believing Him, and sowing your seed, then your days of reaping are sure to come.

A seed will meet any need, but just as a farmer in the natural watches over his seed, so *you* must do some things to guarantee yourself a harvest.

First of all, your life must be one of obedience to God. We please God when we obey Him. We should obey Him simply because He is God and He is our Father. But there are also blessings that come with obeying God: all the benefits of obedience. You can live an abundant, prosperous life here on this earth through obedience, faith, and seed.

The Bible lists many blessings, not just financial blessings, that are available to us when we are obedient to God Almighty.

GALATIANS 3:13,14,29

13 Christ [the Anointed One and His anointing] **hath redeemed us from the curse of the law, being made a curse for us: for it is written, Cursed is every one that hangeth on a tree:**

14 That the blessing of Abraham might come on the Gentiles through Jesus Christ; that we might receive the promise of the Spirit through faith....

29 And if ye be Christ's, then are ye Abraham's seed, and heirs according to the promise.

You may be very familiar with this passage of Scripture, but there are some things we need to be reminded of concerning it, because we can always receive a greater revelation. First of all, this passage tells us that Christ has redeemed us from the curse of the Law. It says that if we are Abraham's seed, then we are heirs according to the promise. So that means if you are

Abraham's seed — and the Bible says you are if you belong to Christ — then you are an heir according to all the promises given to Abraham.

Notice that Christ redeemed us from the Law's curse, because He was made to be a curse for us. He was made a curse for us so that the blessings of Abraham might come on the Gentiles. There are two things we need to understand about this. First, the word *Gentile* doesn't mean *"non-Jewish."* The word *Gentile* means *"without God."* Galatians 3:13-14 could read this way: "Christ has redeemed us from the curse of the Law so that the blessing of Abraham might come on people who are without God."

But we who have accepted Jesus Christ as Savior have found God, and now, though we were once without God, we become Abraham's seed and heirs according to the promise. The blessings may now come on us through Jesus Christ, and we can "receive the promise of the Spirit through faith."

We need to find out what the curse is and what the blessing is.

Since we shouldn't be operating in the curse, which we are redeemed from, it behooves us to know what the curse is that we shouldn't be operating in.

Then we need to know what the blessing is that we *should* be walking in — the blessing that the enemy should not be able to take away from us.

3

1 TIMOTHY 4:8

8   For bodily exercise profiteth little: but godliness is profitable unto all things . . . .

What does *all* mean? *All* means *"everything."* How
much is left after *all?* Nothing.

GODLINESS BRINGS PROFIT

Well, since godliness is profitable unto *all* things,
that means godliness is profitable for your physical
body. Godliness is profitable for your marriage or single
life. Godliness is profitable for your financial well-
being. Godliness is profitable in every single area of
your life. Godly living is profitable.

The Word says in Romans 6:23 that there is a "price
tag" to sin and that the wages of sin is death. God is
against sin, but not because He's against fun. God is
against sin because sin will kill you! It brings death to
you in various ways. Sometimes it can be a slow death.
You don't even recognize you're dying, until — *bang!* —
death catches up to you. But notice again what 1
Timothy 4:8 says:

1 TIMOTHY 4:8

8   . . . godliness is profitable unto all things, having promise
of the life that now is . . . .

"The life that now is" refers to life on this earth. In
other words, godliness has promise. It has blessings for
the life that "now is" on this earth.

BLESSED HERE AND HEREAFTER

That's not all. The rest of verse 8 tells us that the blessings don't stop when we die physically.

1 TIMOTHY 4:8

8 . . . godliness is profitable unto all things, having promise of the life that now is, and of that which is to come.

The blessings of the life that *"now is"* continue in the life that *"is to come."* Christ has redeemed us so that the blessings of Abraham might come on us. Hallelujah!

Let's look at a few of the blessings in the Old Testament, which were a result of obeying God, and a few of the curses, which came from disobeying God.

Now, some people might say, "That doesn't apply to us. That is the Old Testament."

Yes, it's the Old Testament, and it is, indeed, the Law. (The Law is more than just the Ten Commandments. It is the first five books of the Bible — Genesis, Exodus, Leviticus, Numbers, and Deuteronomy — commonly called the Pentateuch.) However, you'll discover that the blessings of Abraham began four hundred years before the Law was even given to Moses.

ABRAHAM'S BLESSING FOR HIS OBEDIENCE

In Genesis 12, God told Abraham to get out of his country and away from his kinfolk unto a land that He would show him. (v. 1.) If Abraham obeyed and did this, God would make him a great nation. And that's exactly what God has done. There are two different nations, or families, on this earth. They are not black and white. The only two families on this earth are those who are of the family of God — those who are born again and members of the kingdom of God — and those who are not.

God also told Abraham that He would bless him if he was obedient. The word *blessed* has several meanings. One of my favorite meanings is *"empowered to prosper"* which is used in The Amplified Bible. So, in other words, God told Abraham, "If you will obey Me, I will empower you to prosper."

Remember, God told Abraham, "I want you to leave your father's house." That meant Abraham had to leave behind his family inheritance and all of his father's wealth and possessions. He had to go out on his own with nothing. But God also said, "I'm going to make you a great nation." Then He said, "I'm going to empower you to prosper." That's the blessing of Abraham. And the Word of God tells us that Abraham's blessings belong to those who are in Christ.

GOD WANTS TO EMPOWER YOU TO PROSPER!

God's intent was not only to make you a member of His kingdom and to make a great nation out of the family of God, but God's intention is also to empower you to prosper.

God went on to say to Abraham, "I'll make your name great, and you shall be a blessing" (v. 2). In other words, God said, "Not only will I empower you to prosper, but you'll be so blessed that you'll be able to empower *others* to prosper."

Deuteronomy 28 lists the blessings for obedience (vv. 1-14), and it also lists the curses that come upon you when you are disobedient. However, Galatians 3 says that Christ came to redeem you from the curse. Thank God, you've been redeemed from the curse — but you haven't been redeemed from the blessing! After reading what the blessing is, it's very easy to see that it's the will of God for you to be empowered to prosper.

So we know that the blessings began before the Law and continued through the Law. The Word of God tells us that we have a better covenant established upon better promises. Jesus is the surety of a new covenant with better blessings! (Heb. 7:22; 8:6.) He makes sure that the blessings of the old covenant, or the Old Testament, are maintained. The blessings weren't done away with. The only thing done away with was the curse.

HEARKEN DILIGENTLY AND BE BLESSED

The blessings that we're about to read in Deuteronomy 28 continue into our covenant and our time — our dispensation. The only way you get under the curse is when you become disobedient. The blessings listed in Deuteronomy 28 belong to believers when

they hearken unto the Lord our God, which means they
are obedient.

DEUTERONOMY 28:1

1   And it shall come to pass, if thou shalt hearken diligently
     unto the voice of the Lord thy God, to observe and to do
     all his commandments which I command thee this day,
     that the Lord thy God will set thee on high above all
     nations of the earth.

The key word here is "diligently." It didn't just say,
"hearken." No, it said, "hearken *diligently.*" There are
people who do what God says every so often. If they
have an emergency or they're in trouble, so they get
right with God. But this Scripture is talking about
someone who lives a *lifestyle* of obedience.

Now, in this verse, God is talking to Israel, saying,
"I'm going to make your nation number one if you
hearken unto what I say." He said all of this because they
were the children of God. We as Christians are also children of God. We are not without God. John 1:12 says,
"But as many as received him, to them gave he power [the
right, privilege, or authority] *to become the sons of God,
even to them that believe on his name."*

So this passage in Deuteronomy 28 is also God
talking to us. He was talking about what He would do
for a nation who obeyed Him. Praise God, we belong to
a nation, a kingdom — and I'm not talking about the
United States of America or some other country — I'm
talking about the kingdom of God!

In Deuteronomy 28:1, God says, "...[I] *the Lord thy
God will set thee on high above all nations of the earth."*

This means that God expects His children to be set on high above all others. He expects that for us, and we can believe Him for it. It belongs to the children of the Lord to be set on high above all others.

YOU CAN BE THE BEST!

Because you are set on high, you can be the best at whatever you do. In fact, you *should* be the best. Of course, to be the best at anything, you have to *strive* to be the best. You have to decide you want to be the best. And you have to continue to do the things necessary to perfect what you do, whatever it may be.

For example, if you're a good pastor, you can always become a better one. If you're a good accountant, you can become a better one. If you're a good computer specialist, you can become an even better one. If you're a mother, you can become a better one. Becoming better comes by asking yourself the question, "How can I get better?" Then never allow yourself to be satisfied with the status quo.

Let's continue in Deuteronomy 28:

DEUTERONOMY 28:2

2   And all these blessings shall come on thee, and overtake thee . . . .

Overtake means the blessings are running after you and will eventually catch you. *Overtake* also implies that the blessings may not be right there with you for a time. But just because they aren't with you right now doesn't mean that they aren't on the way. If you hearken diligently to the Lord your God, the blessings will come.

Don't forget the "diligently" part. People love to read these kinds of verses, but they forget about the fine print in the contract, so to speak, which in this case is "diligently": *"If you will hearken, and do so diligently, then these blessings shall come on you and overtake you."*

Hearken Instantly

Another way I like to say "diligently" is *instantly*. Let's look at it this way. If you are a parent and you tell your child to clean his room, when do you expect him to do it? When he feels like it? When he gets around to it? No, you expect him to do it when you tell him to do it. You might go to his room two hours after you told him to clean it and find that no one's been there. So you yell out, "Didn't I tell you to clean your room?" And he might answer, "I'm coming!" Then five minutes later he still hasn't shown up and has a number of excuses for why he didn't stop what he was doing and proceed directly to his room to clean it up.

As a parent, your reaction to that kind of behavior is not one of pleasure. When your child behaves like that, you are not inclined to bless him. (You might be inclined to spank him!)

I know I am not pleased when my children don't do what I say right away. When they disregard what I tell them to do, I am not so inclined to bless them. Well, then, what in the world makes Christians think that it's okay for them to obey God when they get ready to? They wait until they feel like obeying Him and then expect all His blessings to just fall on them. It doesn't work that way.

What are we talking about here? We're talking about instant obedience to God and His Word.

Following is a summary of the blessings that were to follow obedience to God. They were to follow the children of Israel's hearkening diligently to the Lord their God. (Deut. 28:1.)

DEUTERONOMY 28:3

3   Blessed shalt thou be in the city, and blessed shalt thou be in the field.

It doesn't matter where you go, because wherever it is, you're going to be blessed. If you're in the country, if you're in the city, if you're in Europe, Africa, or Asia, if you're in the north, south, east, or west — wherever you go — you will be blessed.

DEUTERONOMY 28:4

4   Blessed shall be the fruit of thy body. . . .

The "fruit of your body" is your children. You ought to be praying this Scripture over your children and confessing over them, "You are blessed." Confess this even when they don't bring home the right grades from school or don't do what they're supposed to do. Your words should be full of blessing, because your words have power. Your words will become reality in your children's lives. So don't change your confession based on what you see in your children's lives. Continue to say, "The fruit of my body is blessed. My children will follow God."

Verse 4 goes on to say that the "fruit of thy ground" shall also be blessed. The children of Israel lived in an agricultural society. The fruit of their ground was their crops. Their crops were their subsistence — their source of income and how they earned a living. Today you can say, "Blessed shall be my job. I'll be blessed at my job. Blessings will be upon my job."

The Israelites not only cultivated the land, they also took care of livestock. And the rest of Deuteronomy 28:4 says that the fruit of their cattle and their sheep would also be blessed. That is still talking about their jobs and their subsistence.

DEUTERONOMY 28:5

5   Blessed shall be thy basket and thy store.

Whatever the children of Israel did, whatever they crafted, and whatever they put in store was blessed. Everything they set their hand to do was blessed!

DEUTERONOMY 28:6

6   Blessed shalt thou be when thou comest in, and blessed shalt thou be when thou goest out.

You're blessed all the time — in and out, up and down, and round and about! The end result is this: You shall be blessed — if you hearken diligently unto the Lord your God.

DEUTERONOMY 28:7

7   The Lord shall cause thine enemies that rise up against
     thee to be smitten [smacked down!] before thy face: they
     shall come out against thee one way, and flee before thee
     seven ways.

There are going to be enemies that come against
you. There are going to be people who will attack you
for no apparent reason. You'll be trying to think of a
reason they would do something like that to you, and
there won't be any. They may be influenced by a demon
spirit, or they may even be a Christian who yielded to
the devil.

Did you know that Christians can yield to the devil?
Oh, sure, they can. You can yield to the devil just as you
can yield to God. There are Christians who will yield to
the devil and even attack other Christians.

But the blessing says that your enemies may come
against you one way, yet they will flee from you seven ways.

DEUTERONOMY 28:8

8   The Lord shall command the blessing upon thee in thy
     storehouses . . . .

Don't miss the word *command*, because when the
Lord commands something, it is going to happen. In the
beginning, the Lord commanded the light to be, and it
was. It didn't have any choice. The Lord commanded the
fish to swallow Jonah, and it did. And the Lord
commanded the fish to spit him out, and it did.

When the Lord commands something, there's
nothing anyone can do to stop it. Not only does it say,
"The Lord shall command the blessing," it says "in thy

storehouses" - plural. God's assumption is that you will have more than one.

BLESSINGS ON YOUR STOREHOUSES

You're supposed to have more than one bank account. Banks limit how big your account can be, because the FDIC will have to pay a lot of money if something happens to the economy. For instance, if the bank shuts down and you only have insurance up to $100,000, then you will lose any funds you have in one account over $100,000. So you'd better have another account. God said He would bless your storehouses, plural, which means God has more faith in you than you do. The word *storehouses* means barns. A barn is where all the food or substance is kept.

Let's continue reading in verse 8:

DEUTERONOMY 28:8

8   . . . and in all that thou settest thine hand unto . . . .

God will command the blessings on you if you set your hand to a new project or to a new field of work. Some people say, "I'm older, and I've been trained such-and-such way. I can't learn something new." But you can learn to do anything, because God will bless "all that thou settest thine hand unto."

DON'T BE AFRAID TO CHANGE

I know folks who are afraid of computers. They're afraid of trying to learn them because they weren't raised with them. But you can learn anything. You can learn computers. You can learn the ministry. You can learn finances. One constant about success in life is the ability to change, so you have to learn to change. And you have to hearken diligently unto the Lord your God. Then you can go on to any new field, and God said you'd be blessed.

There's still more to verse 8:

DEUTERONOMY 28:8

8 . . . and he shall bless thee in the land which the Lord thy God giveth thee.

Whatever God's given you — whatever house, whatever car, whatever family, whatever career — He said He'll bless it if you will hearken diligently. Diligence is the key to receiving His blessing.

DEUTERONOMY 28:9

9 The Lord shall establish thee an holy people unto himself, as he hath sworn unto thee, if thou shalt keep the commandments of the Lord thy God, and walk in his ways.

We already know that we need to hearken diligently unto the Lord. But this verse goes a little further and says *"...if thou shalt keep the commandments of the Lord thy God, and walk in his ways."* Walking in His ways means you think like Him, talk like Him, see things the way He does, and so forth.

DEUTERONOMY 28:10

10 And all people of the earth shall see that thou art called by the name of the Lord; and they shall be afraid of thee.

When you walk in His ways, everyone will see the hand of God is on you. How? They will see your blessings. They will see that whatever you put your hand to prospers. Whatever change you make gets blessed. Wherever you go, you're blessed. They will see that your storehouses continue to increase and will know that God has something to do with it.

DEUTERONOMY 28:11-13

11 And the Lord shall make thee plenteous in goods, in the fruit of thy body, and in the fruit of thy cattle, and in the fruit of thy ground, in the land which the Lord sware unto thy fathers to give thee.

12 The Lord shall open unto thee his good treasure, the heaven to give the rain unto thy land in his season, and to bless all the work of thine hand: and thou shalt lend unto many nations, and thou shalt not borrow.

13 And the Lord shall make thee the head, and not the tail; and thou shalt be above only, and thou shalt not be beneath; [Here's the fine print] IF that thou hearken unto the commandments of the Lord thy God, which I command thee this day, to observe and to do them.

Notice the phrase *"...and they shall be afraid of thee"* (v. 10). Sometimes a person is afraid of someone because he knows that "there's just something about" that someone he can't figure out, and he doesn't quite know how to react. He might lash out at him because he doesn't understand him, or he might just sit down and be quiet. He might ask another person why that individual is so blessed. People react differently, but that's what this verse is talking about when it says, "They shall be afraid of thee."

God said, "People will see you, they'll see you are blessed of Me, and they'll be afraid of you." Why? Because they will recognize the blessings that are on your life.

DISCOVER, FOLLOW, AND STAY WITH THE PLAN OF GOD FOR YOUR LIFE

To receive the blessings you have to be ready to do the obeying part. And then you have to actually do it. Be ready and willing. If the Lord tells you to go out on the field and teach, and you don't see how you can do it with a wife and kids, just remember that if the Lord told you to do it, He will see you through. If God tells you to do something, that's good enough. You just have to be willing to adjust and adapt and stick with the plan of God.

I remember one time the Lord told me to sell my car in order to downsize financially. So I did it, and I got a much smaller one. Someone might say, "I can't do that. The Lord gave me that car."

I remember a couple in big-time debt that was filing for bankruptcy. They came into my office, and I said to them, "What's the biggest asset you have?" They said,

"Our house." I said, "Sell it and get a smaller one." They replied, "God gave us that house." But that house was bankrupting them.

So I said, "First of all, God didn't give you that house; *you* gave it to you."

"Second, you're out of the will of God because you're heavy in debt and talking about going into bankruptcy. That's stealing from people even if it is legal. A man shouldn't have to wait twenty years to get his money from you. When you buy certain products, you say you are going to pay for them in thirty, sixty, or ninety days, or over the course of four or five years. Then that's what you ought to do. Just repent, sell your house, and down-size for now."

Now, they struggled with that for a while but finally said, "All right." They obeyed God's Word. They sold their house, got the money to pay off their bills, and, later, the Lord gave them another house. The new house was so much better than the one they'd sold, and it was in a far better neighborhood. God blessed them financially, and they didn't have the burden of debt on their backs anymore.

Do What Is Required To Be a Person of Faith

That's what God will do when you obey Him. I always say to people, "Do what's required to be a man of faith, or get out! So many people are stuck on the saying, "I don't want to go backward from where I am now." But, so often, it wasn't the Lord who got them to where they are. The Bible says, *"Except the Lord build the house, they labour in vain that build it. . ."* (Ps. 127:1). In other words, sometimes people build *themselves* up to where they are, and they don't want to go back. But if you're going to follow God, you're going to have to get rid of what you built and let God start you over.

You may suffer a little bit in the natural early on, but if you let God start you over and you stick with it, then your life will start looking a little bit like Deuteronomy 28. It will start happening a little bit at a time. Then it will get to the place where people will start talking about you. They'll say, "There's got to be something wrong with this. They're prospering too much. There's got to be something wrong somewhere." Remember, there's always persecution with the hundredfold return. (Mark 10:30.)

You must maintain constant obedience. That means you have to do what's required. You have to stay in the Word every day. You have to pray in the Spirit every day. You have to do what's required, and you have to stay with it. In some cases, it may take years to get there. People look at the level I'm at now in ministry, but they didn't see me when I was just starting. They didn't see where I came from to get here.

In fact, when I first started in the ministry, people disdained me. They said I was stupid and called me a fool. They were moved by what they saw in the natural, saying, "That brother had a pension working for a great corporation." But, you see, the Lord told me to leave it and start working with Him and to start Word of Faith Church. I obeyed Him, and I have been abundantly blessed. God will do the same for you. Obedience brings the blessing.

C H A P T E R   2

God Has a Place Of Blessing for You!

The verses we read in chapter 1 from Deuteronomy
28 describe blessings, not curses. I mean, that's indis-
putable, isn't it? Why is it, then, that we have people in
the Body of Christ teaching that God does not want His
people blessed, yet right here in the Word, He is blessing
them? We know that the Bible says we have a better
covenant than the Old Testament saints had. If they had
the blessings in their covenant, then we have to have
them in ours.

These blessings were part of the children of Israel's
"promised land." But, remember, in getting into their
actual Promised Land, the children of Israel had to do
several things. They had to hearken unto the Lord; they
had to hear and obey His voice. Second, they had to be
obedient unto the leadership of Moses and, later, Joshua.
Third, they had to be thankful. They weren't allowed to
murmur and complain. (Many of them did, and it got
them killed!)

That's what the children of Israel had to do to get into their Promised Land. They had to get from where they were over into where God wanted them to be. God has a place of blessing for each of us in the Body of Christ that is far beyond where you are now.

YOU CAN BE 'PLENTEOUS' IN STAGES

Verse 11 says, *"And the Lord shall make thee plenteous in goods, in the fruit of thy body, and in the fruit of thy cattle, and in the fruit of thy ground, in the land which the Lord sware unto thy fathers to give thee."* I first started learning about this subject more than twenty-three years ago. When I first read this verse, "plenteous" to me was five hundred dollars.

You have to understand that blessings are relative. Plenteous means different things to different people. That's why at one time, five hundred dollars was plenteous. I'd never had that much money in my hand at one time ever! And storehouses? When I first started out, I didn't have a storehouse. But I noticed that every time I increased, the Word still said the same thing — that I'd be blessed. I'd be obedient to that and go up higher, and every time I did, the Word still said the same thing. So I would go up a little higher, and up and up I would (and still do) continue to go.

"Well," someone might ask, "where does this thing end?" Wherever you decide to stop being diligent and obedient. But if you will be diligent and obedient, then as far as God can go is how far you can go.

Some people don't like to hear teaching about diligence and obedience. But I am where I am today because I was diligent and obedient for the past twenty years. As a result, I get to see people saved and healed. I get to see families restored. It's a tremendous blessing to be doing what I'm doing, but it didn't happen overnight. It came from diligence and obedience — from finding out what God wanted me to do and deciding that what He says is better than anything I can think up.

A LESSON IN HUMILITY

Someone might say, "Well, that's bragging." But walking in the blessings of God is a lesson in humility. People often resist the blessings of God, saying something, such as, "I'm not full of pride." However, it's a statement of pride every time the Word of God says one thing and you decide to do something different.

Verse 12 says, *"The Lord shall open unto thee his good treasure, the heaven to give the rain unto thy land in his season, and to bless all the work of thine hand: and thou shalt lend unto many nations, and thou shalt not borrow."*

Look at the last part of that verse, *"...and thou shalt lend unto many nations, and thou shalt not borrow."* In order to do that, you've got to have some excess. You've got to have some barns, some storehouses. Then you

won't borrow because you won't have to borrow — you
have so much.

Let God 'Make' You

I like verse 13: *"And the Lord shall make thee the
head, and not the tail; and thou shalt be above only, and
thou shalt not be beneath; if that thou hearken unto the
commandments of the Lord thy God, which I command thee
this day, to observe and to do them."* I especially like the
word *make*. The word make implies that God is saying,
"If it isn't so, I'm going to cause it to be anyway"!

DEUTERONOMY 28:14,15

14 And thou shalt not go aside from any of the words which I
command thee this day, to the right hand, or to the left, to
go after other gods to serve them.

15 But it shall come to pass, if thou wilt not hearken unto
the voice of the Lord thy God, to observe to do all his
commandments and his statutes which I command thee
this day; that all these curses shall come upon thee, and
overtake thee.

If you don't obey God curses will be running after
you. They might not have you right now, but they will
catch you and overcome you. The curses break down
into three areas: *poverty, sickness,* and *death.* Poverty is a
curse. It always has been, and it always will be. Sickness
is a curse — always has been, always will be. Death (and
this particularly refers to spiritual death) is a curse —
again, always has been, always will be. A curse is the
result of disobeying the Word of God.

24

What we're talking about in this passage is the whole issue of obedience. Obedience gives us entrance into God's blessings. It gives us the ability to walk in the fullness of Abraham's blessings. God's first blessing to Abraham was to make him rich. Someone asked, "Is the Bible saying we're all going to be millionaires?" No, the word *rich* can be defined as *"a full supply; abundantly provided for."*

After God told Abraham He would make him rich, He went on to tell him, "I'll make you a blessing."

So we know a little something about the blessings of God that will overtake us if we hearken diligently to the Lord our God and if we're obedient. We know, too, that the curses will overtake us if we're not obedient.

PROVERBS 25:12

12   As an earring of gold, and an ornament of fine gold, so is a wise reprover upon an obedient ear.

I like this verse because it aptly describes the attractiveness of obedience. It is a beautiful thing when God has someone who is willing to listen to direction and instruction and who is willing to hear from Him and obey Him.

1 SAMUEL 15:22

22   And Samuel said, Hath the Lord as great delight in burnt offerings and sacrifices, as in obeying the voice of the Lord? Behold, to obey is better than sacrifice, and to hearken than the fat of rams.

To obey God means that you hearken unto the Lord your God and do all that He tells you by His Spirit and by His Word to do. There is no sense in your asking God to speak to you about a matter if you're not doing what's already written in His Word. For instance, in this verse, Samuel was rebuking Saul because Saul did something that he thought was okay even though God had been very specific about what He wanted Saul to do. God rejected Saul as king because of his disobedience.

DON'T GO BEYOND THE WORD

There's no point asking God about something that He's already made clear. For example, you don't have to pray about whether to pay your tithe, because it is already written in the Bible as a command to you. (Mal. 3:10.)

DEUTERONOMY 11:26-28

26 Behold, I set before you this day a blessing and a curse;

27 A blessing, if ye obey the commandments of the Lord your God, which I command you this day:

28 And a curse, if ye will NOT obey the commandments of the Lord your God, but turn aside out of the way which I command you this day, to go after other gods, which ye have not known.

God made it clear. We can choose: blessing or cursing. Now the word *obedience* means *"attentive hearkening; compliance."* It also means *"submission."*[1] Jesus understood this. He said, "I don't do anything, go anywhere, or speak anything unless My Father tells Me." (John 5:19,30; 8:28.) Jesus instantly obeyed His Father. The Bible says in John 16 that the Holy Spirit speaks what He hears the Father saying. (v. 13.) He doesn't decide to say something different. He complies and is in full submission to the Father.

As I said before, the key to obedience and walking in the blessings of God is to have a lifestyle of obedience. You can't say, "Well, I was obedient to do such-and-such one time." No, obedience has to be a *consistent* way of life.

TO TITHE IS A QUALITY DECISION BASED ON OBEDIENCE TO THE WORD

When my wife and I first began our Christian walk, we didn't have enough money to both tithe and pay our bills. So we had to decide whether or not we were going to obey God. We decided to obey God despite what the circumstances were. We didn't always understand how things were going to work out, but we were tremendously blessed, and still are, because of our obedience.

Obedience is a decision. For example, in our marriage, my wife and I agreed early on that divorce was not an option. Everything wasn't always rosy with us, but the decision to obey God puts you in position to get the blessings of God. Without the decision, you will yield to the flesh.

A decision of quality must be made to obey God in everything you do. To obey God's Word is simple because it's God's Word, and that's enough.

A REAL-LIFE TEST OF OBEDIENCE

One time an internationally known minister came to me about going to a certain country that's known for being hostile to Christianity and to the Gospel. I said to her, "Isn't that where two American diplomats got killed just three weeks ago? Isn't that a place where they shout, 'Down with Americans!'? And isn't that a place where they will kill you for being a Christian?"

She said, "Yes. Now let's go."

My head said, *Let her go if she wants to – by herself. The Lord hasn't called you to be an evangelist; He called her. Don't put yourself in there with her.*

The minister told me to pray about it.

Well, I prayed about it, and the Lord said, *Go.* I answered, "Praise You, Jesus." So I told my wife that the Lord told me to go, and I said to her, "You're going to be praying for me while I'm gone, aren't you?"

My wife said, "Where you go, I go."

I got my affairs in order. I knew that if I had missed God, I was going to be in trouble. Ministers from all over the country called us and told us not to go. They told us that we were going to get killed. But the blessings listed in Deuteronomy 28 are for those who diligently and continually do what God says to do. Obedience means you do what He says even when your natural mind doesn't agree or understand.

I told the people who were supposed to travel with me, "I'm releasing all of you. You don't have to go with me. I will go by myself. You don't have to put yourself in harm's way. You all have wives and children, so you don't have to go with me. But I have to go because God told me to go, and I have to obey Him."

To their credit, they all said, "We're going." So they came with me. As soon as we stepped off the plane and went into the building where our bags were supposed to be, we were met by guys with high-powered rifles. Immediately, the devil said to me, *I've got you now. You're dead. You aren't going to get out of here.*

Before we could get to our bags, we had to go through a large crowd of people. These people grabbed us and started going through our pockets. This was all before we even reached our bags! I was thinking, *I obeyed God, and this is what it got me.*

I was concerned about just getting out of the crowd. We were dressed like Americans, and everyone could see the stuff we were carrying with us. People got up in our face as they talked to us, but I thought, *I'm not backing down from the devil!*

The minister who'd invited me didn't back down either. She published an ad for the meeting on the front page of a newspaper there. The ad read, "Jesus is Lord in _____!" It also listed the date, time, and place of the meeting.

In my hotel room before the meeting, I said, "Lord, I have a wife and three children. I have churches I pastor, Lord."

As I started praying, I heard the Lord say to me, *"Being in My will is the safest place you could ever be."*

That's when I relaxed. I said, "Praise God, I'm safe."

We had a tremendous meeting. Thousands of people got saved, healed, and delivered. Whatever we touched was blessed! Today I oversee sixteen churches in that country and they are all prospering.

Now, don't tell me that what you are dealing with is tougher than what I dealt with. I know better. God will prosper whatever you do, wherever you go — if you'll hearken diligently to the voice of the Lord your God and do what He says to do. You must do it over time, not just once or twice, because obedience is a lifestyle.

God may tell you to go somewhere. When you get there, you may say to yourself the same thing I said when I was in that country: "What in the world am I doing here?" But then you get back up on your faith, and before it's over, you understand why God called you there. I was in that country to give hope to those people. They needed someone who would help underwrite the Gospel in that country. Every month we send money to keep the doors open and the pastors preaching there.

OBEDIENCE TO GOD BRINGS GODLY RESULTS!

A year after the initial meeting I held with that minister, we went back and had the largest gathering of any kind — Muslim or Christian. It was the largest gathering ever in the history of the nation. More than 70,000 Muslims got saved and baptized in the Holy Ghost. Blind eyes opened; cripples walked; deaf-mutes heard and spoke. Friend, those are the rewards for obedience!

We've been looking at obedience in the Old Testament. The New Testament also tells you what you have to do to be in a position to receive from God.

1 PETER 1:14-16

14   As obedient children, not fashioning yourselves according to the former lusts in your ignorance:

15   But as he which hath called you is holy, so be ye holy in all manner of conversation [lifestyle];

16   Because it is written, Be ye holy; for I am holy.

People often want me to counsel them, but I really don't have a lot of time to counsel. The truth is, I don't need to counsel, because in very few cases do people actually need counseling. What people need to do is already written in the Word. If they were doing what's already written, they likely wouldn't be in the situations they're in. The way to get out of those scenarios is to do what is written.

FIND 'WHAT IS WRITTEN' FOR YOURSELF

You don't need to sit down across the desk from a pastor to get what is already written in the Word. The only thing most pastors are going to tell you is to turn to the Bible. They'll read you the Scripture. Then they'll tell you to do it. You don't need a pastor to do that for you.

What you need is to get in the Word yourself. Seek God and study the Word. Find out everything God's Word says about your particular situation. Then act on it. Decide to hearken unto the Word of God. Order your mouth and your steps to do it. Then be patient, because you may have dug yourself in deep. It might take a while to get out of your situation, but you'll get out. And when you do, don't get back in again!

The Word of God is clear about financial matters. To prosper you first have to tithe. Then you have to give offerings. Actually, you've never really given until you've tithed. Giving is over and beyond the tithe. (You see, it's tithes *and* offerings.)

Then when you give offerings, believe God and praise Him. The Word of God is clear about these things. It clearly instructs you not to get overwrought in debt. It is also clear about not going into business with unbelievers. The Word of God is clear about working hard unto the Lord and not unto men. That means you should be the first one to get to work in the morning. You shouldn't be the last one to straggle in and punch the time clock and the first one to leave as soon as the clock stops.

Then, if after you've worked hard and honestly for your employer and he comes against you, the Bible says that he'll be cursed but you'll still be blessed.

MAN CANNOT STOP GOD'S BLESSINGS

I was fired from only one job in my entire secular career, and it was through no fault of my own. This particular job was a union job where after you work for ninety days you became a member. Once you became a member of the union they couldn't fire you, but they could fire you any time from day one to day eighty-nine.

For my first performance review, I received a good evaluation. For my next review, I got a promotion. Then, based on that review, I applied for a transfer. They granted me the transfer to a better position with an accompanying higher salary.

Then the regional boss, who had the power to override everyone in command at my office, came down from his office on the eighty-ninth day and fired me. Remember, I would have become a member of the union the very next day. I had just received a promotion and had received nothing but glowing performance reviews.

Now, of course, the flesh told me to retaliate. I'd just gotten married and had no money. My wife didn't have a job. But the Word of God says that vengeance belongs to the Lord. So I could do one of two things: Follow the flesh or follow the Word.

Now before I go on with the story, I want you to understand that this took place in 1975. Both my boss and the regional manager were white males. After I was fired, my boss called me and said, "I can't take it anymore. You are the sixth black male they've fired on the eighty-ninth day. They hire black men in order to get certain benefits. Then they terminate them before they can become part of the union. That's why they fired you, and I'm tired of it. I won't keep my mouth shut about it anymore."

He offered to go to trial with me if I wanted to file a suit against the union. But I told him not to worry about it. The Lord didn't tell me to fight the regional boss or the union. The Lord had told me not to worry about it, so that's what I told my supervisor.

Then God gave me a job in a similar position with Shell Oil Company who shut down its local offices and relocated them to another state only seven months after I began. Then God gave me a tremendous job with IBM. Each time I was forced to change jobs, I was blessed. Because of my performance, I was in position at IBM to move into management when the Lord said to me, *Quit and go to Bible school.*

I obeyed God, and while I was in Bible school, my wife and I received a financial miracle every month. God provided for us supernaturally while we were students. We had debt when we arrived at Bible school, but we graduated debt-free and God sent us out into the ministry debt-free.

Then as soon as we got out into the ministry, we were wronged. The first meeting I held had been booked to last two weeks, but those who'd invited me closed it down after three days because they didn't like what I was preaching — the authority of the believer, understanding our rights in Christ, and walking in joy in the midst of trials. Those were the three messages I had preached when they closed the meeting and literally put me out.

Because I had booked that meeting for two weeks, I didn't have anything else booked. I didn't have a way to support my wife and our young children. Yet God found a way to provide for me, and I kept obeying Him. I have obeyed God for all these years, all the way to where I am today. I am a minister and a pastor of churches in Detroit, Atlanta, and Phoenix.

But you need to understand that success didn't happen overnight. I have been blessed because I was obeying God for all those years. You can read Deuteronomy 28 and read what's happened to me through the years as I've obeyed God.

HOW TO BE BLESSED ALL THE TIME!

Young preachers can preach this message because it's in the Word of God. But I can preach this message because it's in the Word of God and I have lived it. If you want to tell Keith Butler that these things are not so — it's too late. The blessings came and overtook me! I got blessed in the city and blessed in the suburb. I got blessed in the fruit of my body. All of my kids are born again and filled with the Holy Ghost. One is a pastor with me now. The other one is in Bible school, training to be in the ministry. I'm blessed in every way, all the time! I'm convinced that if I opened a church in the middle of downtown Timbuktu, it would prosper! It doesn't matter where I go, I am blessed coming in and going out. That means *all the time!*

When you obey God, "blessed shall be your basket and your store" (Deut. 28:5). "Blessed shall you be when you come in and when you go out" (v. 6). "Your enemies that rise up against you will be smitten before your face" (v. 7). "The Lord shall command the blessing upon you in your storehouses (you need more than one account.) All that you set your hand to will be blessed. The Lord will bless you in the land which He's given to you" (v. 8). In other words, whatever the Lord has spoken to you to do, that is the land He's given you. You shall be blessed in doing it.

"People of the earth shall see that you are called by the name of the Lord, and they shall be afraid of you" (v. 10). "And the Lord shall make you plenteous in goods, in the fruit of your body, and in the fruit of your land, in your promise land" (v. 11). "The Lord shall open unto you His good treasure. (That means you will get rain when you need it.) And all the works of your hands shall be blessed" (v. 12.)

That has been the case in my own life. Some people say, "Well, you're just lucky. Every time you get in a scrape, you come out smelling like a rose!" That's right, and I'm going to *keep on* smelling like a rose, not because I'm something, but because I hearken diligently unto the voice of the Lord God. And I do it *instantly.*

Whatever it is He's called you to do, you can be the best. Whether it be a secretary, musician, or car salesman, you can be the most prosperous. I've seen many people in sales of all kinds become the best in the nation — they did millions of dollars in sales a year. I've seen their businesses boom! I've seen God bless the work of their hands. But it was *after* they obeyed God over and over. They stuck with it over a period of time and saw the result.

People say, "Well, you're a preacher. That's why it works for you." But it doesn't work for just preachers. Come on now, friend. You know thousands of preachers it isn't working for. That's because it has nothing to do with being a preacher. It works for anyone who will stand on the Word of God and stay with it long enough, being diligent and obedient.

You might ask, "How long is that?" Forever! I'm standing on the Word of God forever. His Word is settled in heaven. And it's settled in my heart too. God's Word said it. I believe it. That settles it.

Settle it today in your heart. Settle it today that God's way is the only way that you're going to go. Settle within your heart that there's not an area in your life that can't be scrutinized by the Holy Spirit. There can't be any area in your life where you say, "Oh, God! Don't look at that! Don't go there! I'm not ready!" You have to be ready to do something about your life — your body, your job, your marriage, and so forth. You have to be ready to do whatever God tells you to do. If you will do what He says, you will get the blessings God has for *you*.

THE BLESSING OR THE CURSE?
LEARN TO PUT FIRST THINGS FIRST

We have studied the lists of blessings and curses in Deuteronomy 28. Now I want to show you the difference between people who are operating in the blessings and those who are operating in the curses.

HAGGAI 1:5-8

5   Now therefore thus saith the Lord of hosts; Consider your ways.

6   Ye have sown much, and bring in little, ye eat, but ye have not enough; ye drink, but ye are not filled with drink; ye clothe you, but there is none warm; and he that earneth wages earneth wages to put it into a bag with holes.

7   Thus saith the Lord of hosts; Consider your ways.

8   Go up to the mountain, and bring wood, and build the house; and I will take pleasure in it, and I will be glorified, saith the Lord.

In this passage, God told Israel that they were operating under the curse because they were putting their own personal financial life ahead of carrying out God's will. The curse meant that even though they planted, and even though they worked, they didn't get anywhere. They worked hard and didn't prosper because they had things out of order. So God told them to consider their ways.

After considering their ways, the Israelites stirred themselves up. By Haggai 2, their priorities got in the proper order.

HAGGAI 2:4-7

4   Yet now be strong, O Zerubbabel, saith the Lord; and be strong, O Joshua, son of Josedech, the high priest; and be strong, all ye people of the land, saith the Lord, and work: for I am with you, saith the Lord of hosts:

5   According to the word that I covenanted with you when ye came out of Egypt, so my spirit remaineth among you: fear ye not.

6   For thus saith the Lord of hosts; Yet once, it is a little while, and I will shake the heavens, and the earth, and the sea, and the dry land;

7   And I will shake all nations, and the desire of all nations shall come: and I will fill this house with glory, saith the Lord of hosts.

God said, "When you put My things first and finish My house before you build your own, then I will fill the house with My glory." What is His glory? There are several Hebrew definitions for the word *glory*. One of the meanings is *"that which is good."* The goodness of God is His glory. *Glory* also means *"the manifestation of God's presence."* But there's a third definition of *glory* that people often miss. And I'll show it to you in God's Word.

HAGGAI 2:7-9

7   . . . and I will fill this house with glory, saith the Lord of hosts.

8   The silver is mine, and the gold is mine, saith the Lord of hosts.

9   The glory of this latter house shall be greater than of the former, saith the Lord of hosts: and in this place will I give peace, saith the Lord of hosts.

In verse 7, God says, "I will fill this house with glory." Then in verse 8, He says, "The silver and gold are

Mine." In verse 9, He talks about the glory again. Do you think that God suddenly switched gears between verses 7 and 9? Do you think He was talking about His presence in one verse, gold and silver in the next, and then His presence again in the next? No, He's saying that silver and gold are part of His glory. The house of the Lord was supposed to be the most prosperous place in the nation. Today Christians are the house of the Lord. It is God's will that you walk in His glory on the earth.

PSALM 49:16,17

16 Be not thou afraid when one is made rich, when the glory of his house is increased.

17 For when he dieth he shall carry nothing away: his glory shall not descend after him.

The glory of a man is having the glory of his house increased — to have his finances increase and to be prosperous. Remember, God said, "I'm going to fill My house with My glory." He also said, "You are Abraham's seed, and My promises to Abraham belong to you." You see, God wants to manifest His glory among His children when they have their priorities in order and do what they're supposed to do.

ISAIAH 60:1-5

1 Arise, shine; for thy light is come, and the glory of the Lord is risen upon thee.

2 For, behold, the darkness shall cover the earth, and gross darkness the people: but the Lord shall arise upon thee, and his glory shall be seen upon thee.

3 And the Gentiles shall come to thy light, and kings to the brightness of thy rising.

4   Lift up thine eyes round about, and see: all they gather themselves together, they come to thee: thy sons shall come from far, and thy daughters shall be nursed at thy side.

5   Then thou shalt see, and flow together, and thine heart shall fear, and be enlarged; because the abundance of the sea shall be converted unto thee, the forces of the Gentiles shall come unto thee.

Now, the word *forces* in verse 5 is marked with a little number in my Bible, which tells me that the Hebrew word translated *forces* really means *"wealth."* So we could read this verse as, "The wealth of the Gentiles shall come upon thee."

Part of the glory of God — part of the goodness of God that is manifested by His presence — is financial blessing. God gets pleasure when His children are healed, whole, and have more than enough!

The glory of God should rise and shine among His people. He redeemed us from the curse of the Law — which was first of all poverty. Poverty does not belong among the people of God. Neither does lack nor bankruptcy. If we aren't walking in prosperity, then it's simply because we've missed it. But you don't have to get down in the mouth about it or condemned about missing God.

If you've missed it somewhere, just confess and repent of it, receive your forgiveness, and then act as if what God said is so, because it is. He said in His Word that He has forgiven you and cleansed you. (1 John 1:9.) If you've been forgiven and cleansed, then receive it and praise God. God gets glory when you act as if His Word is true. All of us have missed it in areas in our lives, including the area of finances. But, thank God, we can get it right with God and go on and do what we're supposed to do.

Walking in the Glory of God

We know that Abraham and Isaac were both extremely blessed and walked in the glory of God. I want to show you what Abraham's grandson Jacob did.

GENESIS 30:43

> 43 And the man increased exceedingly and had much cattle, and maidservants, and menservants, and camels, and asses.

Now, remember, man put the chapter divisions in the Bible to help us find specific passages, so we know that the next verse, Genesis 31:1, is a continuation of the same account. You don't begin a completely different, unrelated train of thought with the word *and*.

GENESIS 31:1

> 1 And he [Jacob] heard the words of Laban's sons, saying, Jacob hath taken away all that was our father's; and of that which was our father's hath he gotten all this glory.

This means that the *much cattle, maidservants, camels, and so forth* were considered glory. The glory of God is God's causing you to move away from poverty and into being blessed or empowered to prosper. That's good news!

Now, you might be asking the question, "How do I walk in the glory of God?" It all comes down to obedience.

There are no miracles without obedience. There are three things you must have in order to have your deliverance financially: You must be willing to obey what God said, you must get over into faith, and you must be willing to give your best.

Chapter 3

Obedience, Faith, and Seed

In order to bless you, God requires three things of you: The first is obedience, the second is faith, and the third is a seed. I want to show you how each of these things will bring the blessings of God into your life. When you obey God, walk in faith, and sow seed, your needs will be met supernaturally.

GOD REQUIRES OBEDIENCE

In chapter 1 we looked at some of the blessings that obedience would bring to you. Now let's look a little closer at the subject of obedience.

2 CORINTHIANS 10:3-6

3   For though we walk in the flesh, we do not war after the flesh:

4   (For the weapons of our warfare are not carnal, but mighty through God to the pulling down of strong holds;)

5   Casting down imaginations [human reasonings], and every
     high thing that exalteth itself against the knowledge [or
     Word] of God, and bringing into captivity every thought
     to the obedience of Christ [the Anointed One and His
     anointing];

6   And having in a readiness to revenge all disobedience,
     when your obedience is fulfilled.

2 CORINTHIANS 10:3-6 AMP

3   For though we walk [live] in the flesh, we are not carrying
     on our warfare according to the flesh and using mere
     human weapons.

4   For the weapons of our warfare are not physical (weapons
     of flesh and blood), but they are mighty before God for
     the overthrow and destruction of strongholds.

5   [Inasmuch as we] refute arguments and theories and
     reasonings and every proud and lofty thing that sets itself
     up against the (true) knowledge of God; and we lead
     every thought and purpose away captive into the obedi-
     ence of Christ, the Messiah, the Anointed One,

6   Be in readiness to punish every [insubordinate for his]
     disobedience, when your own submission and obedience
     [as a church] are fully secured and complete.

In these passages Paul is writing to the church at
Corinth. He is teaching them to bring even their
thoughts into the obedience of Christ. You see, obedience begins with you and your own thoughts. If you
don't bring your mind into submission, then you won't
be able to bring your body into submission. Verse 6 tells
us that if we aren't obedient ourselves, we shouldn't be
trying to tell others to be obedient.

The Holy Spirit wouldn't have had Paul tell you to
bring your thoughts into the obedience of Christ if you

didn't have the ability to do it. You can control your mind and your thoughts. Now, I don't mean that you can control what thoughts come into your head. God has access to your mind, but so does Satan. He will shoot his thoughts into your mind. When he does, you have to decide what to do. When any thought comes to your mind, decide if it agrees with the Word of God. If it does, accept the thought as your own. But if it disagrees with the Word of God, tell it to leave and it will have to go. Do not dwell on thoughts that are not in line with the Word of God.

The mind can be a spiritual battleground. To win the battles of the mind, you have to discipline your mind to think in line with God's Word. It starts with a decision. You must decide, *I'm not going to allow my mind to think all kinds of trash. I'm not going to let my mind think bad stuff about people. I'm only going to think on those things which are pure, true, lovely, and so forth.* (Phil. 4:8.)

MATTHEW 6:25,27,28,31

25 Therefore I say unto you, Take no thought for your life, what ye shall eat, or what ye shall drink; nor yet for your body, what ye shall put on. Is not the life more than meat, and the body than raiment?...

27 Which of you by taking thought can add one cubit unto his stature?

28 And why take ye thought for raiment? Consider the lilies of the field, how they grow; they toil not, neither do they spin....

31 Therefore take no thought, saying, What shall we eat? or, What shall we drink? Or, Wherewithal shall we be clothed?

When worrisome thoughts come to your mind, you need to bring them into captivity. All kinds of things may come into your mind, and if you meditate on them long enough, you're going to start talking about them. Once you speak a thought out loud, you have accepted it and it becomes your own. You cannot afford to allow your mind to go its own way. You have to bring every thought into obedience to the Word. It takes work to do that. But when you learn how to discipline your mind, you'll soon learn how to discipline your body. Before long, you will be keeping both your mind and body in obedient submission to God.

JESUS — THE GREATEST EXAMPLE

If you want to have miracles happen in your life, and if you want God to be able to use you to the fullest extent, then you're going to have to learn to be obedient. Jesus, the Anointed One, is the greatest possible example of obedience.

HEBREWS 5:5-9 AMP

5   So too Christ, the Messiah, did not exalt Himself to be made a high priest, but was appointed and exalted by Him Who said to Him, You are My Son, today I have begotten You;

6   As He says also in another place, You are a Priest [appointed] forever after the order (rank) of Melchizedek.

7   In the days of His flesh [Jesus] offered up definite, special petitions [for that which He not only wanted but needed], and supplications, with strong crying and tears,

to Him Who was [always] able to save Him (out) from death, and He was heard because of His reverence toward God — His godly fear, His piety [that is, in that He shrank from the horrors of separation from the bright presence of the Father].

8   Although He was a Son, He learned [active, special] obedience through what He suffered;

9   And [His completed experience] making Him perfect [in equipment], He became the Author and Source of eternal salvation to all those who give heed and obey Him.

This passage tells us that Jesus was not granted His current position simply because He came into the world as the Son of God. Philippians 2 tells us that He became obedient unto death and that is why ". . . God also hath highly exalted him, and given him a name which is above every name: That at the name of Jesus every knee should bow, of things in heaven, and things in earth, and things under the earth; And that every tongue should confess that Jesus Christ is Lord, to the glory of God the Father" (vv. 9-11).

In other words, Jesus was given His high position because He was obedient. Jesus wrapped Himself in human flesh and put aside all of His divine privileges. Everything He did while He was on earth and everything He received from the Father was a result of His obedience. He said that those who would obey God would be blessed too.

If you obey Jesus, you walk in His anointing. He said, "The works I do, you'll do too." (John 14:12.) If you obey Jesus, then you will hear the Father say, "Well done, thou good and faithful servant" (Matt. 25:21).

DEUTERONOMY 8:18-20

18 But thou shalt remember the Lord thy God: for it is he
that giveth thee power to get wealth, that he may establish his covenant which he sware unto thy fathers, as it is
this day.

19 And it shall be, if thou do at all forget the Lord thy God, and
walk after other gods, and serve them, and worship them,
I testify against you this day that ye shall surely perish.

20 As the nations which the Lord destroyeth before your
face, so shall ye perish; because ye would not be obedient
unto the voice of the Lord your God.

These verses tell us what happens when we are not
obedient to God. Destruction is the result of not
obeying God. In my over twenty-five years of ministry,
I've seen marriages and ministries and people perish
simply because people refused to obey God. Instead,
they decided to follow the flesh, and they wound up
getting destroyed.

You have to decide which way you're going to go.
Are you going to live holy before God or not? Are you
going to sleep with someone you're not married to, or
are you going to obey God and His Word? Are you going
to tithe or not? Make up your mind, but remember, in
the long run, disobedience will bring you death.

If you're in need of a miracle today, it's going to cost
you something: obedience.

ISAIAH 1:19

19 If ye be willing and obedient, ye shall eat the good of
the land.

"The good of the land" means you get to have the finest that's out there — if you are willing and obedient. Did you know that a person can be obedient and not be willing? You need both. You have to be willing to sit down when He tells you to sit down and to get up when it's time to get up. You have to be willing to go when you're told to go, and willing to stay when you're told to stay. You have to be willing to open your mouth when you're told to open it, and willing to hold your tongue when He tells you to be quiet. If you willingly do what God tells you to do, you will eat the good of the land.

GOD REQUIRES FAITH

We have seen the importance of obedience, but we need to understand that obedience doesn't work all by itself. Faith must also be active in your life.

ROMANS 16:24-26

24 The grace of our Lord Jesus Christ [the Anointed One] be with you all. Amen.

25 Now to him that is of power to stablish you according to my gospel, and the preaching of Jesus Christ, according to the revelation of the mystery, which was kept secret since the world began,

26 But now is made manifest, and by the scriptures of the prophets, according to the commandment of the everlasting God, made known to all nations for the obedience of faith.

Note that obedience and faith are linked together. This passage of Scripture talks about the obedience of faith, so we know that we can obey God and even do so in faith. The obedience of faith is important in order to receive and maintain a life of miracles and to have your needs met.

LUKE 17:5,6

5 And the apostles said unto the Lord, Increase our faith.

6 And the Lord said, If ye had faith as a grain of mustard seed ye might say unto this sycamine tree, Be thou plucked up by the root, and be thou planted in the sea; and it should obey you.

Jesus uses the term *mustard seed* because it's a small seed, but the important thing to remember is that it's a seed. Your faith is a seed. And what do you do with a seed? You plant it. We see from verse 6 that if you have faith and a seed, then not only will you be obeying, but things will be obeying you. Money will obey you and come to you. Healing will obey you and come to you. Favor will obey you and come to you. Jobs will obey you and come to you.

LUKE 17:7,8

7 But which of you, having a servant plowing or feeding cattle, will say unto him by and by, when he is come from the field, Go and sit down to meat?

8 And will not rather say unto him, Make ready wherewith I may sup, and gird thyself, and serve me, till I have eaten and drunken; and afterward thou shalt eat and drink?

Looking at these verses along with verses 5 and 6, we notice that faith is the servant of the believer. Jesus was saying, in effect, "When you put your faith out in the field, it's working on the problem. When it finishes that problem, don't say, 'Well, sit down, have some coffee, and relax.'" No, when your faith comes back victorious from working on that problem, send it out to work on another one. In other words, always keep your faith at work. Always obey God. And always be sowing seed in the field.

If you will do those three things, you will decree a thing and it will come to pass. (Job 22:28.) You will speak, and it shall be so. Speak to that *sycamine tree* (Luke 17:6.) Speak to that empty bank book, that sore throat, that wayward husband or wife — speak to whatever your problem is — and the power of God will go to work on your behalf because you spoke. You will have what you say. (Mark 11:23.)

If you're disobedient, then nothing will obey you — including your own words. But if you are obedient, your words will cause your problems to obey you. Obedience in faith is the key.

FAITH AND A PROSPEROUS SOUL

The Bible says that faith comes by hearing, and hearing by the Word of God. (Rom. 10:17.) It also says not to be conformed to this world, but to *"...be ye transformed by the renewing of your mind..."* (Rom. 12:2). The apostle John said something else about the soul of man, which is the mind, will, and emotions.

3 JOHN 2

2 Beloved, I wish above all things that thou mayest prosper and be in health, even as thy soul prospereth.

We know from this verse that your health and your finances are the two areas that Satan will attack the most. This verse says that God's will is that we prosper and be in health, but notice it also says, *as thy soul prospereth*. That means that if your soul isn't prospering, then you aren't going to prosper or be in health.

As I said, the soul is the mind, will, and the very seat of the emotions. Rev. Kenneth E. Hagin always says, in effect, "Right thinking produces right believing and right confession, which produces right action, which produces right results." You have to think right to speak right, to act right, and to have right. The way you have to think is, *It's God's will for me to prosper, and it's God's will for me to be in health. I've been redeemed from the curse. That curse is poverty, sickness, and spiritual death.*

Therefore, meditate on the Word so that your mind will be renewed to think in line with the Word of God.

GOD REQUIRES A SEED

The Bible gives many examples of God's requiring obedience, faith, and seed from His children. As we already saw in some detail, one great example is that of Moses and the Israelites' deliverance from Egypt.

In Exodus 12, we can read about their deliverance. We know that the children of Israel were in bondage for more than 400 years when God sent them a deliverer by the name of Moses.

In Exodus 5, God had given Moses certain instructions to follow. Moses went to Pharaoh and told him, "Let my people go. They need to go spend three days in the wilderness because they have to sacrifice and worship and give praise unto God." But, immediately, when Moses obeyed God by going to Pharaoh, things got worse for the Israelites.

WORSE AT THE FIRST

Pharaoh told Moses, "I'm not going to let them go. Instead, I'm going to make things even harder for them. I'm going to require that they continue to make their same quota of bricks, but I'm not going to give them any straw to make the bricks with. They're going to have to get their own straw." Then Pharaoh had all the elders of Israel beaten.

Sometimes when you obey God, things seem to get *worse at the first*. That's what happened to the Israelites. Then, because Pharaoh wouldn't let the children of Israel go, Egypt endured nine plagues. I mean, some of the worst kinds of things you could imagine came upon them — plagues of frogs, plagues of lice, their water turned into blood, a hailstorm arose that was so bad it killed every living thing that was outside, including the crops in the fields. But after all nine plagues, Pharaoh still wouldn't let God's people go.

Then God said to Moses, "This time he's going to let them go." But this time God would require something of the children of Israel. With all the other plagues, He didn't require anything of Israel. But for the last plague, He required something of them in order for them to be let go.

EXODUS 12:1-10

1   And the Lord spake unto Moses and Aaron in the land of Egypt, saying,

2   This month shall be unto you the beginning of months: it shall be the first month of the year to you.

3   Speak ye unto all the congregation of Israel, saying, In the tenth day of this month they shall take to them every man a lamb, according to the house of their fathers, a lamb for an house:

4   And if the household be too little for the lamb, let him and his neighbour next unto his house take it according to the number of the souls; every man according to his eating shall make your count for the lamb.

5   Your lamb shall be without blemish, a male of the first year: ye shall take it out from the sheep, or from the goats:

6   And ye shall keep it up until the fourteenth day of the same month: and the whole assembly of the congregation of Israel shall kill it in the evening.

7   And they shall take of the blood, and strike it on the two side posts and on the upper door post of the houses, wherein they shall eat it.

8   And they shall eat the flesh in that night, roast with fire, and unleavened bread; and with bitter herbs they shall eat it.

9   Eat not of it raw, nor sodden at all with water, but roast with fire; his head with his legs, and with the purtinence thereof.

10 And ye shall let nothing of it remain until the morning;
and that which remaineth of it until the morning ye shall
burn with fire.

Now, remember, God had said, "Pharaoh will let you
go this time." Then He commanded them, "I want you
to take a lamb." The Israelites were slaves in Egypt, and,
just as it's been throughout history, they didn't have
much as slaves. When you are a slave, all you're allowed
to have is enough to keep you alive. So the children of
Israel didn't have very much. They may have had a few
goats and lambs and maybe a little acreage so they could
plant food and eat, but that was it.

GOD WANTS YOUR BEST SEED

In Exodus 12:1-10, God was saying to the Israelites,
"I want you to plant a seed. I want you to give Me your
best lamb, a one-year-old lamb that is without blemish. I
want you to sacrifice it unto Me."

I know for some people that had to be a hard word
because after nine plagues, I'm sure some of the
Israelites were talking. (People then were no different
than people now.) I can hear some of the people saying,
"Now, wait a minute. Moses said Pharaoh was going to
let us go before. He said that after the first plague, and it
didn't happen. He said that after the fifth plague, and it
didn't happen. He said that after the ninth plague, and it
didn't happen. Now He wants us to take our very best

lambs — that's all we've got! And He wants us to kill them and roast them with fire?"

Not only did God say for them to do that, but He said, "I want you to take the lamb, pour its blood into a basin, and then take the blood and deface your houses with it."

I can hear an Israelite wife saying, "I finally got this house the way I want it, and God wants me to deface it by putting blood all over the front of it?"

God was requiring that the Israelites give a seed and in giving that seed, they had to be obedient. He'd said, "I want you to kill your best lamb. Then I want you to take the blood of the lamb and put it over the doorposts. Then I want you to roast that lamb with fire and eat it — all of it. I want you to eat the head and the hind parts."

I will tell you, I don't mind lamb chops. I don't mind a little roast of lamb or a little leg of lamb. But, man, when you start talking about eating the hind parts and the head and the feet — I don't know about all that! But God said to eat the whole lamb and to eat bitter herbs along with it. He also said, "I want you to get dressed up like you're ready to go!"

I'm sure that at this point they had to feel stupid. They're going to kill their prize lamb, deface their house with blood, eat bitter herbs that don't taste good, and eat all the parts of the lamb. Then they're going to put on their hat, their boots, their coat, and all their traveling clothes. Everyone in the house is going to be standing up, ready to go. Now, I know they felt stupid doing all that.

The Lord has told me over the years to do a number of things that seemed crazy to me at first. They didn't seem to make any sense, and sometimes I felt stupid doing them. You may feel stupid doing what God told you to do, but don't be moved by what you feel. Just obey.

What God required of Israel didn't seem to make much sense. When Israel was in need, God instructed them to give, and the seed they gave reaped a harvest of deliverance. Their seed of a lamb didn't bring them a lamb in return. Instead, it set them free, because a seed will meet any need.

Remember the way it works: obedience, faith, and seed. You must have all three working in your life, because there aren't any shortcuts.

CHAPTER 4

Streams of Anointing

There are four streams of anointing, or blessings, that the Israelites received because they obeyed God and by faith gave their best lamb as a seed. As you begin to obey God and plant seed in faith, then you, too, will experience these streams of anointing.

THE FIRST STREAM: PROTECTION

The first stream of anointing, or blessing, they received was supernatural protection. They were protected because they were obedient unto God. In the case of their exodus from Egypt, God required them to give a seed, and they did. Then when Death came by, it passed over the houses marked by the blood of the lamb.

I firmly believe that whatever bad weather comes to my area, it will not hit my house. It might hit all around me and level everyone else's house, but it won't hit my property because I am a big-time seeder and a man of faith. How can I say that? God protected the Israelites' homes because of their obedience, faith, and seed. He is the same God today, and the same anointing of protection is upon my life because of my obedience, faith, and seed.

THE SECOND STREAM: FAVOR

The second stream of anointing the children of Israel received was favor. Favor is an anointing that comes from God. Favor is worth gold; it is a big-time something. When you have God-inspired favor with the right person at the right time, the only thing that can happen to you is promotion. God will give you favor with your enemies. Egypt was Israel's enemy, but God gave them favor with the Egyptians.

In Exodus 3, God told Moses what would happen after Israel obeyed God, acted in faith, and sowed their seed.

EXODUS 3:21,22

21 And I [the Lord] will give this people favour in the sight of the Egyptians: and it shall come to pass, that, when ye go, ye shall not go empty:

22 But every woman shall borrow of her neighbour, and of her that sojourneth in her house, jewels of silver, and jewels of gold, and raiment: and ye shall put them upon your sons, and upon your daughters; and ye shall spoil the Egyptians.

The Amplified Bible says, "You shall not go empty-handed. But every woman shall [insistently] solicit of her neighbor, and of her that may be residing at her house, jewels and articles of silver and gold, and garments, which you shall put on your sons and daughters; and you shall strip the Egyptians [of belongings due to you]" (vv. 21,22).

Psalm 105 says they went out with silver and gold. But, remember, they first had to give seed. They had to be obedient, and they had to walk in faith. They had to walk up to the Egyptian masters and say, "Give me your silver, give me your gold, and give me your clothes."

Think of it: The Egyptians' cattle are dead, they don't have drinking water, and they are suffering from horrible plagues, all because of the children of Israel. Yet God gives the Israelites favor with their masters, and when God's people tell them, "Give me your gold, give me your silver, and give me your clothes," the Egyptians say, "Okay!"

Something supernatural must have come over them to make them say, "Yes, I have to give you my gold. And yes, I have to give you my silver. And here's my best dress. Here, take this one. And take *that* one." Hallelujah!

EXODUS 12:35,36

35 And the children of Israel did according to the word of Moses; and they borrowed of the Egyptians jewels of silver, and jewels of gold, and raiment:

36 And the Lord gave the people favour in the sight of the Egyptians, so that they lent unto them such things as they required. And they spoiled the Egyptians.

Do you need favor? It's about time to start believing God for it. Do you plant seed? Do you obey God? If you do, then you ought to believe God for favor. Some people might say, "They won't like me because I'm this color or that." But it doesn't have anything to do with your color. The issue is having favor with the right person at the right time, and God will give you that. It's not so much having favor with man, such as a banker or an official at City Hall. No, it's having favor with *God* that counts.

It seems people look for excuses why they can't get something done. They blame republicans, democrats, city folk, and suburban folk. But I'm telling you, you and God are a majority.

The Bible says that Jesus had favor with God and man. (Luke 2:52.) God will also give you favor because of your seed. He will give you so much favor that even people who are unsaved and have never been to church will start giving you things, no strings attached. You might say, "I can't imagine anything like that happening to me." That's your problem. It's about time that you start seeing what God did for others and believe that what He did for them He will also do for you.

The children of Israel were servants of God. But because of Jesus, we are sons of God too. You are in a higher spiritual position than they were, so if God did something for them, you know He will do it for you.

LUKE 6:38

38 Give, and it shall be given unto you; good measure, pressed down, and shaken together, and running over, shall men give unto your bosom. For with the same measure that ye mete withal it shall be measured unto you again.

God doesn't send money down from heaven. He doesn't have any counterfeit presses up there. The blessings from God always come through man. However, you must be a giver in order to be a receiver. With the same measure you give, you shall receive. It happened for the children of Israel, and it can happen for you too.

EXODUS 12:36

36 And the Lord gave the people favour in the sight of the Egyptians, so that they lent unto them such things as they required. And they spoiled the Egyptians.

This verse says the children of Israel *spoiled* the Egyptians. That doesn't mean they got just a little bit of silver and a little bit of gold and took one dress. No, they wiped out the Egyptians' belongings. Israel got all of it!

Why did Israel have favor with the Egyptians? Why did the Egyptians let Israel take their silver and gold? God put such favor for the Israelites inside the Egyptians that the Egyptians just let them do it.

It was the anointing. The anointing will remove every burden and destroy every yoke. The Israelites had a burden of poverty and oppression and lack. But God's anointing removed those burdens and met their need in an instant. Israel walked out loaded with Egypt's silver and gold.

PSALM 105:38

38 Egypt was glad when they departed: for the fear of them fell upon them.

Then not only did God give the children of Israel favor with the Egyptians, but He instilled in the

Egyptians a fear of Israel. I tell you, the sinner ought to be afraid of the Christian. They ought to be so afraid that they decide to join up! They ought to have the attitude, "You sure can't beat the righteous, so we'd better join them."

THE THIRD STREAM: HEALING

The third stream of anointing that the Israelites received because of their seed was healing.

PSALM 105:37

37 **He brought them forth with silver and gold: and there was not one feeble person among the tribes.**

This verse says that there was not one feeble person. That means that every person received strength and healing. So when you give, don't just believe for money to be returned to you, because the same power that will get finances to you will heal you from the crown of your head to the soles of your feet. Money is important, but getting rid of sickness and disease — especially a terminal disease, such as cancer — is more important.

THE FOURTH STREAM: PROVISION

The fourth stream of anointing that the children of Israel received because of their seed was provision. God not only delivered them from the land of Egypt, but He took care of them once they were freed from slavery.

PSALM 105:39

39 He spread a cloud for a covering; and fire to give light in
the night.

The Israelites were out in the hot desert wilderness,
so God said, "I'm going to be your shade while you are
out there." God was their cloud during the daytime so
that they wouldn't get too hot. At night, when they
needed light, God said, "I'll be your light from heaven."
What brought this provision? Their seed did.

PSALM 105:40

40 The people asked, and he brought quails, and satisfied
them with the bread of heaven.

Imagine three million people lugging gold and silver
around in the wilderness. There aren't any shops in the
desert, so why did God load them up with riches? God
wanted them to know that whether or not they had gold
or silver, He is still the One who provides for their needs.

They had all of Egypt's money but nowhere to spend
it. They had no place to buy food. But God, their
Provider, spoke to the quails, saying, "Dive down. Lay
yourself down and die." By doing so, millions of quails
became food for the Israelites.

The Israelites needed something to go along with the
quail dinner, so God gave them bread from heaven twice
a day. Well, if you're eating a two-piece quail dinner with
rolls, you need something to wash it down with! So God
gave them water. Out of one rock He gave enough water
to quench the thirst of three million people. That's
eleven million gallons of water a day — out of a rock.

YOUR SEED AND THE MEASURE OF ANOINTING YOU WALK IN IS YOUR DECISION

After seeing what God did for the children of Israel, don't tell me that God can't meet your need. Every day eleven million gallons of water were given to the Israelites from a rock. So what is an electric bill, a gas bill, or a grocery bill to Him?

Some people want the church to give them benevolence money to pay their rent and other bills. But God didn't tell us to lean on the arm of man or on the church and to take tithe and offering money that's supposed to go to preaching the Gospel and use it to pay our bills. That's not the job of the local church. I tell you, it's our job to get on the Word for ourselves. God has no lack of food, clothing, money, or anything we need. But we have to give our seed. We can't be tipping God and expecting the blessings to fall on us when our hearts and attitudes aren't right.

I'm not unsympathetic to people who find themselves in bad financial situations. I've been in bad financial situations myself. But I gave myself out of it. That's why I'm convinced that a seed will meet any and every need. It doesn't even matter what your seed is. It doesn't have to be money. I gave pencils and shoelaces when I didn't have any money.

I've been there. I've been through tests and trials and poverty and lack. But I stood on the Word of God. Someone said, "Well, everybody can't be like you." Tell me why not! It's the same salvation, the same Word, the same faith, and the same Jesus. The salvation that God provided for me is no different than the salvation He's provided for you. You have to be tenacious. It's up to you. You are one decision away from having your miracle become a reality in your life.

But you have to give seed. You have to get your faith up and then do what you ought to do. The streams of anointing that the Israelites experienced are available to you today. All it takes is seed, obedience, and faith to tap into the flow.

We read in Exodus how God delivered the children of Israel from Egypt and caused them to walk in the streams of anointing that we've looked at in this chapter.

Psalm 105 tells us that one reason God delivered them was because He remembered His promise to Abraham. Abraham had been a man of obedience, faith, and seed. God remembered that and honored his descendants.

PSALM 105:42,43

42 For he remembered his holy promise, and Abraham his servant.

43 And he brought forth his people with joy and his chosen with gladness.

God brought His people out with joy! The word *gladness* means *"they came out with singing."* They came out with joy. They carried all that gold and silver, and they were singing, "The Lord is good all the time!"

It began with their obedience, their faith, and their seed. All the Israelites were asking for was just to be delivered from Egypt. But God's a "too much" God. He's a "good measure, pressed down, shaken together, running over" God (Luke 6:38). He gave the children of Israel protection, favor, healing, and provision, and He is well able to do the same for *you*. Your seed sown in obedience and faith will meet any need you have.

CHAPTER 5

The Law of Genesis

If you sow good seed in faith with the right motive, you can be sure that it will produce a harvest. But what kind of harvest will you reap?

In the natural realm, we find the law of Genesis in operation, which says that everything produces after its own kind. For example, if you cut open an apple, you will find apple seeds inside. You will not find orange seeds or watermelon seeds. The Word says that everything produces after its own kind, and that the seed is in itself. (Gen. 1:11.)

We know that's certainly true. Cats produce cats, and dogs produce dogs. And I don't care what scientists may say, monkeys produce monkeys; monkeys don't produce people. People produce people. Sometimes people produce people who act like monkeys, but that's only because no one disciplined them when they were children (but that's another subject altogether!). We know that horses don't produce tigers, and apples don't produce oranges. Everything produces after its own kind. That's the law of Genesis.

GENESIS 1:11,12

11 And God said, Let the earth bring forth grass, the herb yielding seed, and the fruit tree yielding fruit after his kind, whose seed is in itself, upon the earth: and it was so.

12 And the earth brought forth grass, and herb yielding seed after his kind, and the tree yielding fruit, whose seed was in itself, after his kind: and God saw that it was good.

The fact that everything produces after its own kind is the natural flow of the earth. In Genesis 8:22 the Lord God Almighty says, "As long as the earth remains, seed-time and harvest, cold, and winter shall not cease."

Well, that's true in the earth. Everything does produce after its own kind. But, thank God, giving is not bound to just the natural laws of this earth. The law of Genesis does not apply when you get over into the realm of the spirit. When you get over into exercising faith, which is a spiritual act, you supersede natural law. Jesus said, "My words are spirit, and they are life" (John 6:63). When you act on God's words and on what God said to do, you supersede natural law.

One of the definitions of *El Shaddai* is *"one who can supersede all natural laws."* God can speed things up, and He can slow things down. He can do something totally different than the way it's always been done. The laws of nature don't bind *El-Shaddai*.

HEBREWS 7:8

8 And here men that die receive tithes; but there he [Jesus] receiveth them, of whom it is witnessed that he liveth.

We are still witnessing that Jesus is not dead, but alive. It says that when men receive tithes given on the earth, Jesus also receives them. So the tithe is not just a physical act; it's also a spiritual act. It gets over into the realm of the spirit. It will supersede the natural law of Genesis, the law that says everything produces after its own kind.

In other words, when you sow a seed, you won't necessarily get back the thing that you have sown. If you sow money, and you don't need money, then what good would it do you to reap only money? The law of Genesis does not apply to the realm of the spirit. Instead, the spiritual laws of tithing and giving supersede the natural laws of sowing and reaping. When you give a seed, you can reap whatever it is that you need at the time.

A JOB FOR EL-SHADDAI

A perfect example of spiritual laws superseding natural laws is found in 2 Kings 4. When the Shunammite woman gave to Elisha, the prophet of God, her need was met. The Bible says she was already a rich woman, so a lack of money was not her problem. She wanted to have a baby. In the natural, it was impossible, because her husband was so old he was physically not able to reproduce. The natural laws of reproduction made having a baby impossible. So when that Shunammite woman acted upon the Word of God, it was a job for El-Shaddai.

2 KINGS 4:8 AMP

8   One day Elisha went on the Shunem, where a rich and
     influential woman lived who insisted on his eating a
     meal. Afterward whenever he passed by he stopped there
     for a meal.

This woman was very rich. Every time Elisha the
prophet of God came to town, she fed him. Then finally
she suggested to her husband that they add a room onto
their house so Elisha could stay there while he was in
Shunem. (v. 10.) It goes without saying that putting an
additional room on a house costs money. If you build on
a room for someone, that's a monetary gift.

After Elisha received the woman's gift, he asked her
what she wanted God to do for her in return. She told him
that she was well taken care of and didn't need anything.
Then the prophet told his servant to find out what the
woman needed. The servant came and told Elisha that
the woman was "without child" (2 Kings 4:8-14).

The Scripture says her husband was old. Now, there
are a lot of old people mentioned in the Bible, but you
don't find very many places where it reads in the same
sentence, "She doesn't have a child; her husband is very
old." This boy must have been really old!

During those days, if a woman went childless, she
considered herself to be cursed. This Shunammite's need
was not money; her need was a child. Her need was for
the power of God to come on that husband and to cause
his "youth to be renewed like the eagle's".

Elisha told her, "...*About this season* [or the same
time next year], *according to the time of life, thou shalt*

embrace a son..." (v. 16). The power of God must have come on her husband, because one year later, she had a bouncing baby boy. Her seed opened the door for her need to be met.

This woman's monetary seed did not produce after its own kind; she did not receive money in return for financial seed. No, but because that seed was sown in faith, the seed supernaturally met her need. She gave finances and received a child.

PROVISION FROM UNEXPECTED CHANNELS

Remember the story of the Israelites in Exodus 12? They did what God told them to do and sowed their best lamb as a seed. This act was one of obedience and faith, so spiritual laws governed their sowing and reaping. The children of Israel sowed a lamb, but they reaped deliverance, protection, favor, healing, and provision.

Your seed will also meet every need, but your seed, obedience, and faith depend on you. It's a decision that you will have to make. I told myself over twenty-five years ago that the Word of God was either true or it wasn't — it either worked or it didn't. I decided to believe the Word of God. I acted and stayed on the Word, and God supernaturally paid off every bill I had until I was debt-free. I have been an individual with major debt, and I have also been debt-free. Let me tell you that debt-free is better.

When the children of Israel were parched and thirsty,
God opened a rock and water gushed out like a river
into the dry places. (Exod. 17:6.) The Israelites probably
never thought God would use a rock to provide water
for them, because people don't normally get water out
of a rock. But, remember, El Shaddai is One who can
supersede nature or natural laws, and a seed will meet
any need.

If you have some dry places in your life, God has
water. Quit looking to the normal way for God to get
things done for you. God can get money to you in spite
of your job and in spite of your paycheck. God can get
healing to you in spite of what the doctor has said. He is
El-Shaddai, and He can do whatever He wants to do. He
can get your answer to you through ways you've never
thought or dreamed of. He is God Almighty.

I want you to notice what happens when you do
what God says to do. The children of Israel, enslaved in
Egypt, gave sacrificially and obeyed God. They exercised
their faith. Instead of crying and looking for man to
meet their need, they relied on God, and He delivered
them from Egypt and from the hands of Pharaoh. It took
the Israelites years to finally get to the Promised Land,
but they eventually got there. Some people have to hit
rock bottom before they decide to stick their heels in the
ground and fight faith's fight.

It's time for you to stick your heels in the ground
and tell the devil, "I'm not going to accept this anymore.
I know what my rights are, and I'm standing on the

Word of God. I'm not moved by what I see. I'm not moved by what I feel. I'm moved only by what I believe, and I believe the Word of God."

God has never failed me, and He won't fail you, either. The Israelites got their miracle, their silver and gold, their healing, their deliverance, their quail, their manna, and their water. God brought them forth with joy and gladness. The word *gladness* means *"singing."* They came out with joy, and they were singing. You don't have to wait until you get out of your situation to have joy. You can believe what God has said and have joy now.

THE LAW OF THE SPIRIT

Remember, when you operate in the realm of the spirit, you are subject to the laws of the spirit, which means supernatural things are going to happen to you: supernatural deliverance, supernatural protection, supernatural healing, supernatural favor, supernatural provision, and so forth.

PSALM 105:44

44 And [God] gave them the lands of the heathen: and they inherited the labour of the people.

This verse tells us that the heathen did all the work, and God's children got all the benefits. When they finally entered the Promised Land and got over into Jericho and those other nations, the cities were already built and the lands already farmed. Everything they needed was just sitting there waiting for them. They didn't do one thing except walk in and take it.

God has whatever you need. He has healing, a husband, a wife, cars, houses — whatever you need. It's time to obey God and sow your seed. Give Him your best. Get in faith and believe that a seed will meet any need, and that includes whatever *you* need.

The Right Way To Give

The children of Israel received divine protection, favor, healing, and provision because of the seed they sowed. If the seed you sow is good and it's planted in good ground, then it will produce. But you also have to sow your seed with the right motives.

You need to understand the proper way to give. You don't give just to get something from God. You cannot buy the blessings and anointing of God. In Acts 8, we have the account of Simon the magician trying to do this very thing. When he tried to buy the blessings of God, the apostle Peter told him, "Your money perish with you, because you've thought that the blessings of God may be purchased with money" (Acts 8:20).

So, you see, giving must always be done from a right heart and a right spirit. There are people who give for the wrong reasons, but just because that happens, don't "throw the baby out with the bath water." Just throw out the dirty bath water — keep the baby! In other words,

don't you stop giving just because someone else gives
with the wrong motives.

Not only must you give with the right motives, but
you must give good seed. God doesn't want what you
have left over. He wants the first fruits. God doesn't want
a polluted offering; He wants the best you have to offer.

MALACHI 1:6-10

6   A son honoureth his father, and a servant his master: if
     then I be a father, where is mine honour? and if I be a
     master, where is my fear? saith the Lord of hosts unto
     you, O priests, that despise my name. And ye say,
     Wherein have we despised thy name?

7   Ye offer polluted bread upon mine altar; and ye say,
     Wherein have we polluted thee? In that ye say, The table
     of the Lord is contemptible.

8   And if ye offer the blind for sacrifice, is it not evil? and if
     ye offer the lame and sick, is it not evil? offer it now unto
     thy governor; will he be pleased with thee, or accept thy
     person? saith the Lord of hosts.

9   And now, I pray you, beseech God that he will be gracious
     unto us: this hath been by your means: will he regard
     your persons? saith the Lord of hosts.

10 Who is there even among you that would shut the doors
     for nought? neither do ye kindle fire on mine altar for
     nought. I have no pleasure in you, saith the Lord of hosts,
     neither will I accept an offering at your hand.

This passage of Scripture is first of all talking about
preachers. God requires those who are in the ministry to
give properly before preaching on giving to others. I am
the biggest giver in my church. I'm not going to let
anyone give bigger than I do. Why? Because I'm the
leader, and I lead by example. I'm not one of those

preachers who preaches about tithing and then doesn't tithe. I'm the first one to tithe and the first one to give.

Some people might say, "Yes, of course, you can give big. Look at the position you're in." But where were they when my income was less than $6,000 a year? I was still a tither and a giver then. And where were they when I didn't have any food in the cupboard? I still tithed. Where were they when I had more bills than I had money to pay? I tithed anyway. That's how I got to be where I am today.

GIVE GOD YOUR BEST

The word *best* implies a variety of things: *top; purest; finest; superior.* Instead of giving their best lamb as an offering on the altar to God, the priests in Malachi 1 gave Him one that was diseased. (As if God wouldn't notice!) And instead of giving God the finest shewbread, they gave Him polluted bread.

Yes, they gave an offering, but it wasn't their best, and God knew the difference. God knows the difference between what is your best — what is superior — and what your flesh is comfortable giving.

God told them, "You despise Me." That is strong language. He said, "You despise My Name, and you are saying that the table of the Lord is contemptible." In other words, they were speaking against the offering: "Why do we have to give these offerings? How come we have to give so much in the offering? Why can't God be satisfied with this? How come He has to ask for the very best lamb we've got, the best bread we've got, the best everything? Why does He have to have the best? Doesn't He know that hurts us? We can't afford that."

That's what they were saying. And God said, "You have contempt for My table."

The times haven't changed. People are still doing the same thing. Some might say, "I'm not giving my money to those preachers. They're just lining their pockets."

First of all, whether the preacher is lining his or her pockets or not, God is still going to hold you responsible for whether you did what He said in His Word you should do. You can't allow that to be an excuse for not doing what you are supposed to do, because God will not accept excuses.

Of course, a preacher shouldn't be lining his or her pockets, but let God judge the preacher who is doing that. James 3:1 says, ". . . *be not many masters, knowing that we shall receive the greater condemnation.*" I feel sorry for the preacher who misuses the money that God gives him or her through the people in the church. The preacher will pay big time for that. Hell fire is going to be mighty hot for that person. Personally, there is no amount of money worth hell fire!

Notice what God said in Malachi 1:8. He said, in effect, "If you brought this diseased stuff and this polluted bread to the head of your government, do you think he would be pleased? And yet you bring it to

Me." You wouldn't take your second-best stuff to someone of importance, would you? No, you wouldn't, especially if you thought that person could be a great blessing to you.

Then God went on to say, "If the governor, a mere man, wouldn't receive it, then don't expect Me to receive it." God told them He wasn't going to accept their offering.

Many times, what people don't recognize is, the quality of seed they give is the quality of their return. I'm not talking about amounts. Remember what Jesus said in Mark 12 about the woman who gave two "mites" in the collection plate. The rich men put large sums of money in the offering, yet Jesus said that she gave more than they did. You see, Jesus was talking about the quality of her seed; she gave the best that she could give.

Sometimes God may require of us more than we think we can give. He thinks our best is more than we think it is. Why? Because God knows what is truly our best. He wants to get you out of the natural and over into faith. Giving what is comfortable to your flesh is not your best. There is no faith in that. Faith is when you get over into "deep water."

OFFERINGS THAT ARE WELL-PLEASING TO GOD

In the following passage of Scripture, the apostle Paul describes offerings given by the Philippian church

that were well-pleasing to the Father, because the
Philippians gave their best.

PHILIPPIANS 4:15-18 AMP

15 And you Philippians yourselves well know that in the
early days of the Gospel ministry, when I left Macedonia,
no church (assembly) entered into partnership with me
and opened up [a debit and credit] account in giving and
receiving except you only.

16 For even in Thessalonica you sent [me contributions] for
my needs, not only once but a second time.

17 Not that I seek or am eager for [your] gift, but I do seek and
am eager for the fruit which increases to your credit [the
harvest of blessing that is accumulating to your account].

18 But I have [your full payment] and more; I have everything I need and am amply supplied, now that I have
received from Epaphroditus the gifts you sent me. [They
are the] fragrant odor [of] an offering and sacrifice which
God welcomes and in which He delights.

In the *King James* version of the Bible, verse 18
reads, *"But I have all, and abound: I am full, having
received of Epaphroditus the things which were sent from
you, an odour of a sweet smell, a sacrifice acceptable,
wellpleasing to God."* When you are doing something
that is well-pleasing to God, what do you think God is
going to do? He is going to command His blessings
upon you.

The only other place in the Scripture where I've seen
"well-pleasing" mentioned in this context is when Jesus
was being baptized in the Jordan River. The heavens
opened, the Spirit of God descended like a dove, and

God said, "This is My beloved Son, in whom I am well pleased" (Matt. 3:17; Mark 1:11; Luke 3:22).

We know then that the Word of God puts giving on the same level as Jesus' commitment and obedience. No wonder the devil has tried to make "giving" a nasty word. Satan knows that if you are well-pleasing to God, then you will get over into what Jesus got. After God said, "This is My beloved Son, in whom I am well pleased," it says in Luke 4:14 that Jesus came out of the wilderness in the power of the Spirit.

Let's look again at the offerings the Philippians gave that were well-pleasing to God.

PHILIPPIANS 4:15,19 AMP

15 And you Philippians yourselves well know that in the early days of the Gospel ministry, when I left Macedonia, no church (assembly) entered into partnership with me and opened up [a debit and credit] account in giving and receiving except you only....

19 And my God will liberally supply (fill to the full) your every need according to His riches in glory in Christ Jesus.

In verse 15, Paul is commending the Philippians on their partnership with him in the area of finances. He said that no one had entered into partnership with him financially except the Philippians. *Partnership* is a word modern churches aren't too familiar with. Partnership is not just a one-time action. Partnership means that you join with someone until the job is done.

A marriage is supposed to be a partnership. A marriage is supposed to be "until death do us part." It is not supposed to be "until I get tired of you" or "until you get older and don't look quite as good as you used to." No, in a marriage, the husband and wife are partners in everything until life is over. When I married my wife, I swore to God that I would stay with her until either she goes or I go — and I wasn't talking about to court.

You need to understand that where the work of the kingdom of God is concerned, there are partnerships. Most modern church people aren't partners; they're "tippers." Some Christians tip God at their church. They give God a tip instead of giving Him their best. They tip Him and then expect His power and blessings to be poured out on them. It doesn't work that way. When you don't give God your best, you will get the same thing that the people got in Malachi. God will say, "You despise Me, and you consider giving contemptible. Therefore, I won't accept your offering," which means you might as well have kept it.

A seed will meet any need, but each individual has to decide for himself what he's going to do. He's either going to be with God or not. He's going to get on the Word and stick with it or not. He's either going to walk in faith or he's not. Great things will happen when you are consistently obedient to God and you give seed in faith.

As I said, offerings should be given in faith — as an act of faith. Preachers should never have to make a pull for money in church. The reason why ministers do so is because people aren't doing what God is telling them to do. God is speaking to them, and they won't do it, so the minister is going to the flesh. I refuse to do that. I want my people to be blessed, and they aren't going to be blessed if I pull for money, because then it would be of coercion and not of faith. So I refuse to do it. Pulling for money is not going to do them any good. Personally, pulling for money is contemptible.

When people give with the right spirit and in accordance with the Word of God, it is an act of faith. The reason you are blessed when you give is not because you give to be blessed, but because your giving is an act of faith that opens the door for God to come in and bless you. When you give, God is then able to flow through to any area where you may have a need and bless you.

CHAPTER 7

A Seed Will Meet Any Need!

We have looked at the differences between the law of Genesis, which says that everything produces after its own kind, and the laws of the spirit, which are not bound by natural laws. We know that the spiritual law of sowing and reaping is not bound by the natural law of Genesis.

I want you to know beyond a shadow of a doubt that a seed sown in faith will reap a harvest that supersedes the natural law of Genesis and will meet the need — whatever it is — of the sower.

THE WOMAN WITH THE ALABASTER BOX

Let's go through the Bible and read different accounts of a seed meeting any need. I want to build my case for you. (I once aspired to be a lawyer, but the Lord changed my course in life.) I want to build it so airtight, the "jury" will have to say, "We've got the right verdict!"

The first example from the Bible is the woman with
the alabaster box who washed Jesus' feet with her tears.
This account is written in the Gospel of Luke and the
Gospel of Matthew. I want to look at both accounts to
help prove that a seed will meet any need.

LUKE 7:36,37

36   And one of the Pharisees desired him [Jesus] that he
     would eat with him. And he went into the Pharisee's
     house, and sat down to meat.

37   And, behold, a woman in the city, which was a sinner,
     when she knew that Jesus sat at meat in the Pharisee's
     house, brought an alabaster box of ointment.

MATTHEW 26:6-9

6   Now when Jesus was in Bethany, in the house of Simon
    the leper,

7   There came unto him a woman having an alabaster box of
    very precious ointment, and poured it on his head, as he
    sat at meat.

8   But when his disciples saw it, they had indignation,
    saying, To what purpose is this waste?

9   For this ointment might have been sold for much, and
    given to the poor.

Matthew gives us a better description of this ointment in the alabaster box. He said it was a very precious
ointment. So, obviously, whatever ointment was in the
alabaster box, it wasn't cheap stuff; it was the real thing.
It was something expensive.

Now let's go back to Luke 7 again and read a little
further.

LUKE 7:37-44,46

37 And, behold, a woman in the city, which was a sinner,
    when she knew that Jesus sat at meat in the Pharisee's
    house, brought an alabaster box of ointment,

38 And stood at his feet behind him weeping, and began to
    wash his feet with tears, and did wipe them with the hairs
    of her head, and kissed his feet, and anointed them with
    the ointment.

39 Now when the Pharisee which had bidden him saw it, he
    spake within himself, saying, This man, if he were a
    prophet, would have known who and what manner of
    woman this is that toucheth him: for she is a sinner.

40 And Jesus answering said unto him, Simon, I have some-
    what to say unto thee. And he saith, Master, say on.

41 There was a certain creditor which had two debtors: the
    one owed five hundred pence, and the other fifty.

42 And when they had nothing to pay, he frankly forgave
    them both. Tell me therefore, which of them will love
    him most?

43 Simon answered and said, I suppose that he, to whom
    he forgave most. And he said unto him, Thou hast
    rightly judged.

44 And he turned to the woman, and said unto Simon, Seest
    thou this woman? I entered into thine house, thou gavest
    me no water . . . .

46 My head with oil thou didst not anoint: but this woman
    hath anointed my feet with ointment.

The Amplified Bible says, "You did not anoint My
head with [cheap, ordinary] oil, but she has anointed
My feet with [costly, rare] perfume" (v. 46).

LUKE 7:47-50

47 Wherefore I say unto thee, Her sins, which are many, are
forgiven; for she loved much: but to whom little is
forgiven, the same loveth little.

48 And he said unto her, Thy sins are forgiven.

49 And they that sat at meat with him began to say within
themselves, Who is this that forgiveth sins also?

50 And he said to the woman, thy faith hath saved thee; go
in peace.

First, notice that Jesus said that this woman's giving
was an act of faith. Second, notice that this woman
came with some precious ointment and began to wash
the feet of Jesus. She brought expensive perfume, and
her need was met. But guess what need was met? She
didn't have a financial need. Her need was to be forgiven.
She brought precious ointment — a seed of monetary
value — and she walked out forgiven of her sins.

ZACCHAEUS

Our next example of a seed meeting any need is
also found in the Gospels and deals with a rich man
named Zacchaeus.

LUKE 19:1-8

1 And Jesus entered and passed through Jericho.

2 And, behold, there was a man named Zacchaeus, which
was the chief among the publicans, and he was rich.

3 And he sought to see Jesus who he was; and could not for
the press, because he was little of stature.

4   And he ran before, and climbed up into a sycamore tree to see him: for he was to pass that way.

5   And when Jesus came to the place, he looked up, and saw him, and said unto him, Zacchaeus, make haste, and come down; for to day I must abide at thy house.

6   And he made haste, and came down, and received him joyfully.

7   And when they saw it, they all murmured, saying, That he was gone to be guest with a man that is a sinner.

8   And Zacchaeus stood, and said unto the Lord; Behold, Lord, the half of my goods I give to the poor; and if I have taken any thing from any man by false accusation, I restore him fourfold.

Zacchaeus said, "I'm rich. And, Lord, I'm going to give half of what I have to the poor." Or, in other words, he was saying, "I'm giving my seed unto You. And if there's anyone I've done wrong to, I'm going to make it up four times."

Well, if Zacchaeus had the finances to do that, then the man didn't need money, because he had plenty. But he still planted the seed.

Notice what Jesus' reply was to Zacchaeus.

LUKE 19:9

9   And Jesus said unto him, This day is salvation come to this house forsomuch as he also is a son of Abraham.

Praise God, Zacchaeus's seed met his need! In this case, his need wasn't monetary; he had some other needs. He needed to receive salvation. And the Master met his need.

THE CENTURION

Our third example is also found in the Gospels, in Luke 7.

LUKE 7:1-5

1   Now when he [Jesus] had ended all his sayings in the audience of the people, he entered into Capernaum.

2   And a certain centurion's servant, who was dear unto him, was sick, and ready to die.

3   And when he heard of Jesus, he sent unto him the elders of the Jews, beseeching him that he would come and heal his servant.

4   And when they came to Jesus, they besought him instantly, saying, That he was worthy for whom he should do this:

5   For he loveth our nation, and he hath built us a synagogue.

The Amplified Bible says, "For he loves our nation, and he built us our synagogue [at his own expense]" (v. 5). This man was also wealthy. He had built the Jewish people a church with money out of his own pocket. He gave a seed unto the children of Israel, and look at what happened as a result.

LUKE 7:6-8

6   Then Jesus went with them [the centurion's messengers, the elders of the Jews]. And when he was now not far from the house, the centurion sent friends to him, saying unto him, Lord, trouble not thyself: for I am not worthy that thou shouldest enter under my roof:

7   Wherefore neither thought I myself worthy to come unto thee: but say in a word and my servant shall be healed.

8   For I also am a man set under authority, having under me soldiers, and I say unto one, Go, and he goeth; and to another, Come, and he cometh; and to my servant, Do this, and he doeth it.

The centurion believed that if Jesus would just speak the word, then his servant would be healed.

Jesus said, *"...I have not found so great faith, no, not in Israel"* (v. 9).

I want you to notice what put the man in position for his faith to work. He gave a seed, but his need wasn't a financial need. His need was for something other than money. The need he had was for his servant to be healed. And his need was met because a seed will meet any need.

THE MAN WITH THE PALSY
AND HIS FOUR FRIENDS

Let's look at yet another example of a financial seed meeting a need other than a financial need.

MARK 2:1-4

1   And again he [Jesus] entered into Capernaum after some days; and it was noised that he was in the house.

2   And straightway many were gathered together, insomuch that there was no room to receive them, no, not so much as about the door: and he preached the word unto them.

3   And they come unto him, bringing one sick of the palsy, which was borne of four.

4   And when they could not come nigh unto him for the press, they uncovered the roof where he was: and when

> they had broken it up, they let down the bed wherein the
> sick of the palsy lay.

This is the story about the man with palsy and the four men who brought their friend to be healed by Jesus. It says they couldn't get in through the door where Jesus was teaching, because the house was jam-packed and people were standing all around the front door.

So one of the four got the idea to tear a hole in the roof of the house and lower the sick man down on his bed through the hole. Now, when you break up someone's roof, you are going to have pay for that roof. (If you get up on my house and tear up my roof, you're going to pay for it!)

You see, those men were willing to pay whatever price was necessary in order for their friend to get his need met. They tore up that roof knowing that they were going to have to pay for it later. Their act of faith was going to cost them some money. But the Bible says that when Jesus saw their faith, He said, "Your sins are forgiven you. Take up thy bed and walk" (vv. 5,11). Because these men sowed a seed in faith, their friend was healed. They sowed the seed, and Jesus met the need.

THE QUEEN OF SHEBA

Looking in the Old Testament, we find another example of a seed meeting any need. The queen of Sheba had heard of the famous King Solomon. But according to 1 Kings 10:1, she didn't just hear about Solomon; she heard about Solomon in connection with his God. (That's what people ought to hear about you too. They ought to hear about you in connection with your God.)

The queen of Sheba came to Solomon to prove him with hard questions. But notice she didn't just come to Jerusalem; she came to Jerusalem with something. She came with a seed.

1 KINGS 10:1-3

1   And when the queen of Sheba heard of the fame of Solomon concerning the name of the Lord, she came to prove him with hard questions.

2   And she came to Jerusalem with a very great train, with camels that bare spices, and very much gold, and precious stones: and when she was come to Solomon, she communed with him of all that was in her heart.

3   And Solomon told her all her questions: there was not any thing hid from the king, which he told her not.

When she came to get her questions answered, the queen didn't come empty-handed. She brought a very great train of gold, a very great train of spices, and a very great train of precious stones. She was in serious need, so she brought some serious seed. She needed to know how to run the nation she was ruling. She needed some wisdom and understanding, and the Lord provided through Solomon, a man of God, all that she needed.

Since nothing was hidden from Solomon, then Someone must have been supplying him with all the answers. It was God Almighty who revealed unto Solomon the answers that the queen of Sheba needed.

The queen's seed brought her wisdom and under-standing, and it gave her the opportunity to spend time with a great man. The Bible says, *"A man's gift maketh room for him, and bringeth him before great men"* (Prov. 18:16). She went before the greatest man on the planet at that time. Her seed put her in position to see how he operated his kingdom. She received a lesson that served her the rest of her days.

Not only did the queen's seed bring her before the wisest man on earth who was able to give her all the answers that she needed, but before she left to return to Sheba, Solomon told her to take anything she wanted out of his royal bounty. The king's bounty is where he stores all of the riches that his army plunders from defeated nations. So money came to her when she planted that seed. But it wasn't just money that came to her, because her need was even greater than money. She received answers to hard questions. Her seed met her need.

SOLOMON

Solomon was a man of God who obediently and faithfully offered sacrifices unto the Lord. One night the Lord appeared to him in a dream and said, "Ask what I shall give you, and it will be given you" (1 Kings 3:5). God told Solomon he could have whatever he wanted, and He didn't put any limits on the offer. He said, "Ask Me for whatever you want."

Look at how Solomon answered the Lord.

1 KINGS 3:6-9

6   And Solomon said, Thou hast shewed unto thy servant David my father great mercy, according as he walked before thee in truth, and in righteousness, and in uprightness of heart with thee; and thou hast kept for him this great kindness, that thou hast given him a son to sit on his throne, as it is this day.

7   And now, O Lord my God, thou hast made thy servant king instead of David my father: and I am but a little child: I know not how to go out or come in.

8   And thy servant is in the midst of thy people which thou hast chosen, a great people, that cannot be numbered nor counted for multitude.

9   Give therefore thy servant an understanding heart to judge thy people, that I may discern between good and bad: for who is able to judge this thy so great a people?

When God had said, "Ask Me for whatever you want," Solomon could have asked for riches or long life or the destruction of his enemies. But, instead, he asked for wisdom so that he could minister to his people.

Look at what God said in reply.

1 KINGS 3:12,13

12   Behold, I have done according to thy words: lo, I have given thee a wise and an understanding heart; so that there was none like thee before thee, neither after thee shall any arise like unto thee.

13   And I have also given thee that which thou hast not asked, both riches, and honour: so that there shall not be any among the kings like unto thee all thy days.

Solomon was a man who gave seed all of his life by offering sacrifices unto the Lord. Then when he was told he could have whatsoever he desired, he sowed a seed into Israel's future by asking God for wisdom instead of riches. He put the nation of Israel before himself. In return, God said, "I'm going to give you riches. I'm going to give you the silver and gold. I'm also going to give you the wisdom and understanding you've asked Me for." The seed that Solomon planted opened the door for his need to be met. His need was to have wisdom and understanding so that he could do his job.

SIMON PETER

As you probably know, Simon Peter was a fisherman by trade. You're probably familiar with the story in Luke 5 of Peter and his men fishing all night and catching nothing. But that was before Peter's seed met his need!

LUKE 5:1-3

1 And it came to pass, that, as the people pressed upon him [Jesus] to hear the word of God, he stood by the lake of Gennesaret,

2 And saw two ships standing by the lake: but the fishermen were gone out of them, and were washing their nets.

3 And he entered into one of the ships, which was Simon's, and prayed him that he would thrust out a little from the land. And he sat down, and taught the people out of the ship.

In verse 3, it says that Peter allowed Jesus the use of his fishing boat. After Jesus had used the boat, He did something for Peter in return. He told Peter to go out and cast his nets into the deep, even though Peter had been fishing all night long and had caught nothing.

When Peter obeyed Jesus and cast his net, he hauled in such a load of fish that his net broke!

LUKE 5:4-7

4   Now when he had left speaking, he said unto Simon, Launch out into the deep, and let down your nets for a draught.

5   And Simon answering said unto him, Master, we have toiled all the night, and have taken nothing: nevertheless at thy word I will let down the net.

6   And when they had this done, they inclosed a great multitude of fishes: and their net brake.

7   And they beckoned unto their partners, which were in the other ship, that they should come and help them. And they came, and filled both the ships, so that they began to sink.

Notice that Peter didn't do exactly what Jesus told him to do. Jesus had said, "Let down your nets." *Nets* is plural. But it says Peter let down *the net*, singular. And just that one net got them so many fish that the fish filled two boats, and the boats began to sink.

I want you to see something else in this passage. When Peter gave Jesus the use of his boat, it cost him something. It cost him his time, and it cost him the wear and tear of his boat. It cost his fishermen and the people helping him their time — time they could have spent fishing and making money. So Peter was sowing a financial seed. Yes, he received fish in return, and fish was money to him. But he got something more than that: Jesus called him into the ministry and said, "Now I will teach you to fish for men" (Luke 5:10). Peter's seed put him in position to receive all that God had for him.

CORNELIUS

Cornelius was a big-time prayer and a big-time giver. This is a man who didn't have a financial need, but he did have a need.

ACTS 10:1-4

1   There was a certain man in Caesarea called Cornelius, a centurion of the band called the Italian band,

2   A devout man, and one that feared God with all his house, which gave much alms to the people, and prayed to God alway.

3   He saw in a vision evidently about the ninth hour of the day an angel of God coming in to him, and saying unto him, Cornelius.

4   And when he looked on him, he was afraid, and said, What is it, Lord? And he said unto him, Thy prayers and thine alms are come up for a memorial before God.

Cornelius gave to the poor; he gave alms. God recognized his financial seed and rewarded him by telling him how to get the Gospel preached unto him. An angel said to Cornelius, "...Thy prayers and thine alms are come up for a memorial before God. And now send men to Joppa, and call for one Simon, whose surname is Peter: He lodgeth with one Simon a tanner, whose house is by the sea side: he shall tell thee what thou oughtest to do" (vv. 4-6). God was saying, "You send men down there so I can show you what it is I have for you."

God was speaking to Peter at the same time. He told Peter not to call unclean what He has called clean. (Acts 10:10-16.) While God was revealing this to him,

Cornelius and his friends showed up. God said to Peter, "Arise and go with them, doubting nothing: for I have sent them" (v. 20).

Peter recognized that he was supposed to preach the Word to these Gentiles, whom God had called "clean." So he began to preach Acts 10:38, "How God anointed Jesus of Nazareth with the Holy Ghost and with power: who went about doing good, and healing all that oppressed of the devil..."

As Peter began to speak, the Holy Ghost fell on them who heard the Word.

ACTS 10:44,45

44   While Peter yet spake these words, the Holy Ghost fell on all them which heard the word.

45   And they of the circumcision which believed were astonished, as many as came with Peter, because that on the Gentiles also was poured out the gift of the Holy Ghost.

Cornelius was the first Gentile to receive the Holy Ghost. His need wasn't money; his need was to get filled with the power of God. Cornelius gave a financial seed, and he received the Holy Ghost. A seed will meet any need.

Someone might ask, "Wait a minute. You're trying to say that you can buy the power and blessings of God?"

Most definitely not! Remember from Acts 8 what happened when Simon tried to do that very thing.

ACTS 8:18-21

18   And when Simon saw that through laying on of the apostles' hands the Holy Ghost was given, he offered them money,

19 Saying, Give me also this power, that on whomsoever I lay hands, he may receive the Holy Ghost.

20 But Peter said unto him, Thy money perish with thee, because thou hast thought that the gift of God may be purchased with money.

21 Thou hast neither part nor lot in this matter: for thy heart is not right in the sight of God.

Simon had said, "Man, I want to buy the opportunity, the power, to lay hands on people that they may be filled with the Holy Ghost." And he was told, "No. Your heart is not right with God for asking such a thing. Your money perish with you, because you can't buy the power of God."

You can't buy the power of God, but I will tell you one thing. God will do anything to get you in position where He can bless you. Your seed will meet any need, whatever it is.

GOD WANTS TO BLESS US

Nearly everyone is familiar with the story of Job. Job lost everything — his family, his possessions, and his health. His body was broken out with sores — he had boils all over his body, from head to toe. His three friends kept telling him, "God must have done this to you. God is the One messing you up. You must have sinned. You must repent. God is doing all of this."

But God spoke up and said, "You've spoken wrong things about Me. You'd better go ask Job to pray for you." (Job 42:7-9.)

God didn't have to tell them to go to Job and ask him to pray for them. He could have just told them to repent right then and there, and they would have. And God's compassion would have been there. But God wanted to do a "two-for-one special." In other words, He didn't want just to bless Job's friends, He also wanted to do something for Job. So God got Job to pray. And the minute Job got over into a little bit of faith, God turned Job's captivity. (Job 42:10.)

God is just looking for a reason to bless you. He is looking for something that will allow Him to come in and turn your captivity. He wants to make a difference in your life. He needs your seed, because a seed will meet any need.

WHAT ARE TRUE RICHES?

In this book, I've been talking about the fact that a financial seed will meet any need in your life, whether it be a need for salvation, healing, deliverance, wisdom, improved family relationships, or money. Whatever the need, your seed sown in faith and obedience will meet it.

People often identify money with riches and vice-versa. But in Luke 16, Jesus tells us what true riches are, as well as how to handle what we think of as riches:

money. In the following verses, we see how important it is to handle money the right way — God's way.

LUKE 16:10,11

10 He that is faithful in that which is least is faithful also in much: and he that is unjust in the least is unjust also in much.

11 If therefore ye have not been faithful in the unrighteous mammon [mammon is money], who will commit to your trust the true riches?

Jesus said, in effect, "If you don't handle money right, what in the world makes you think you're going to be able to handle the true riches?" That begs the question: What are the true riches? The true riches are the spirit of wisdom, understanding and power — the Spirit of the Lord. True riches include the anointing of God, the power, and the Spirit of God. The true riches is the anointing of God that will lift our burdens and destroy every yoke.

If you can't handle money properly, what in the world makes you think you're going to be able to have the true riches made manifested unto you? You see, the right-handling of money will release the power of God. Wrong-handling of money will stop the power of God.

REMEMBER ISRAEL

In Exodus 12 we saw the obedience and faith of Israel in receiving their deliverance. They took their best lamb and gave it to God as seed. Their right-handling of money released for them the true riches — the anointing and power of God to deliver them from Egypt's clutches. Then in faith and obedience to God, they poured the blood of their lamb in a basin, defaced their house with it, ate bitter herbs and lamb, and then put on their traveling clothes! They walked out with protection, favor, healing, and provision, or wealth. A seed will meet any need!

'MY GOD SHALL SUPPLY ALL YOUR NEED'

Let's talk some more about sowing seed, about giving. Did you know that giving is an act of love? Giving is a God-kind of action; it is being like God. What heaven is, is manifested on the earth when you give. The money that you give causes someone else to be free and to walk in liberty.

PHILIPPIANS 4:15-19

15 Now ye Philippians know also, that in the beginning of the gospel, when I departed from Macedonia, no church communicated with me as concerning giving and receiving, but ye only.

16 For even in Thessalonica ye sent once and again unto my necessity.

17 Not because I desire a gift: but I desire fruit that may abound to your account.

18 But I have all, and abound: I am full, having received of Epaphroditus the things which were sent from you, an odour of a sweet smell, a sacrifice acceptable, wellpleasing to God.

19 But my God shall supply all your needs according to his riches in glory by Christ Jesus.

He'll supply all your needs, not just your financial needs. Yes, that's where it starts. When you sow financial seed, money will come. But your blessing won't stop with money. A husband will come to you. A wife will come to you. A baby will come to you. Joy will come to you. Favor will come to you. Blessings will come to you. Whatever you need will come to you!

God will supply all your needs according to His riches in glory by the anointing that's on Jesus. It's the same anointing that will remove your burdens and destroy every yoke. So if you need money, you can say, "Money cometh!" and "Money, thou art loosed!" If you need a baby, you can say, "Baby cometh!" and "Baby, thou art loosed!" If you need favor, you can say, "Favor cometh!" and, "Favor, thou art loosed!" If you need a husband, you can say, "Husband cometh!" and "Husband, thou art loosed!" A seed will meet any need.

What kind of need do you have? You might have all kind of seed out there, planted, just believing for the financial return. Well, keep on doing that, because you will get money. But don't limit God there. Yes, money cometh, but believe for healing too. Believe for favor too. Believe for the husband or wife too. Believe for the child too.

You may have been believing for money as you've sown your seed, but, now, switch gears a little bit, because that seed is supernatural. It wasn't sown in the natural realm. It doesn't produce only after its kind; it produces in every single area — wherever you are willing to believe.

If you need healing in your body, release your faith for healing. If you need favor, release your faith for favor. If you need a mate, release your faith for that husband or wife. If the doctors told you that you can't have a baby, release your faith for a bouncing baby boy or girl.

SUDDENLY!

Remember what happened to that Shunammite in 2 Kings 4? God moved in His customary way — *suddenly!* Suddenly, something happened to that old man. Suddenly, the anointing came on him. Power came on him, and his wife had a bouncing baby boy.

Whatever you need, your seed will bring it. Suddenly, you'll be healed. Suddenly, you'll be delivered. Suddenly, you'll have favor. Suddenly, doors will open for you. Suddenly, you'll be pregnant. Suddenly, the anointing of God will lift all your burdens and destroy the yoke of bondage.

The word *suddenly* means *"quickly"* or *"at once."* But the "Keith Butler" translation defines it as: One second, things are one way, and the next second, everything is changed!

So when you give your seed, you might be poor
right now, but, in a second, everything can be changed.
You might be sick right now, but, in a second, you could
find yourself well in body. You may not have a baby
right now, but, in a second, you could be pregnant.

The Lord will make a way because of the seed.

PHILIPPIANS 4:19

19 But my God shall supply all your need according to his
riches in glory by Christ Jesus.

I used to think the word *but* didn't belong in this
verse. Let's look at it along with verse 18.

PHILIPPIANS 4:18,19

18 But I [Paul] have all, and abound: I am full, having
received of Epaphroditus the things which were sent from
you, an odour of a sweet smell, a sacrifice acceptable,
wellpleasing to God.

19 But my God shall supply all your need according to his
riches in glory by Christ Jesus.

I always thought verse 19 should say, *"And* my
God...." (Some translations do use the word *and.*) But,
no, God was making a point. The word is supposed to
be *but.* Paul was saying, "Yes, I know you gave money.
You gave a financial gift. *But,* my God will supply *whatever* needs you have. Your seed will meet *any* need!"

CHAPTER 8

Seed Time and Harvest

We've learned that a seed will meet any need; however, there are a few more things I want you to understand about the way seed time and harvest — sowing and reaping — works.

PSALM 105:37-45

37 He [the Lord] brought them forth also with silver and gold: and there was not one feeble person among their tribes.

38 Egypt was glad when they departed: for the fear of them fell upon them.

39 He spread a cloud for a covering; and fire to give light in the night.

40 The people asked, and he brought quails, and satisfied them with the bread of heaven.

41 He opened the rock, and the waters gushed out; they ran in the dry places like a river.

42 For he remembered his holy promise, and Abraham his servant.

43 And he brought forth his people with joy, and his chosen with gladness:

44 And gave them the lands of the heathen: and they inherited the labour of the people;

45 That they might observe his statutes, and keep his laws. Praise ye the Lord.

Notice the word *satisfied* in verse 40. When God gets involved with something, He doesn't just tip and dip a little bit here and there. With God, it's not "a little dab will do you". No, when God meets your need, you are *satisfied*.

We have read a number of Scriptures, and we've found that when you get over into the realm of giving, which is planting a financial seed into the kingdom of God, then that seed supersedes the normal law of Genesis — the normal law of how seeds operate in the earth. However, in the kingdom of God, when you get into the realm of faith and plant seed, it will produce in any area of need that you have.

THE SEED IS SUPERNATURAL

We looked at many people in the Word of God who sowed seed and were healed, had children, and had spiritual needs met. There were all kinds of areas in which the seed produced, because the seed is supernatural.

Now, I want to answer the question, "How far will the seed go?" Or, in other words, how long will the seed last? How far will its effect reach? Let's go to the Word of God and find out.

In the natural realm, a seed will normally produce one for one. But in the realm of the spirit, a seed can go on for decades. One seed can produce a multiplicity of results for a period of time that your brain can't fathom. As long as the quality of the seed is your best and you remain obedient and in faith, your seed will produce and will keep on producing.

DON'T GIVE UP ON YOUR SEED

Remember, seed time and harvest is not an overnight process. In the natural, you don't plant one day and reap the next. You could plant a seed and have a harvest pop up years later when the need arises. You might not have a particular need when you plant, but when the need arises, up comes that harvest.

A seed will meet any need, regardless of how long it is before the need shows up. So have patience with your seed, and don't give up on it.

ACTS 10:1-4

1   There was a certain man in Caesarea called Cornelius, a centurion of the band called the Italian band,

2   A devout man, and one that feared God with all his house, which gave much alms to the people, and prayed to God alway.

3   He saw in a vision evidently about the ninth hour of the day an angel of God coming in to him, and saying unto him, Cornelius.

4   And when he looked on him, he was afraid, and said,
     What is it, Lord? And he said unto him, Thy prayers and
     thine alms are come up for a memorial before God.

Do you remember this guy, Cornelius, a big-time
prayer and a big-time giver? His prayers and alms went
up before God as a memorial.

The word *memorial* means *"record"* and *"reminder"*.
Cornelius's seed and his prayers reminded God to keep
His promise. Cornelius wasn't a one-time giver or a one-
time prayer. No, he gave and prayed consistently.

Verse 2 says, "alway." Cornelius was *always* giving
seed, but his need wasn't met immediately. Yet Cornelius
didn't stop praying or giving. He didn't give up on his seed.

The angel told him that his prayers and seed
reminded God to meet his need. Cornelius's seed not
only caused him to be saved and filled with the Holy
Ghost, but it caused his whole family, all of his friends,
and all of his workers to be saved and filled with the
Holy Ghost.

A seed will meet any need. And if God chooses to
operate in the gifts of the Spirit by having an angel
appear unto you, He will do whatever it takes to meet
your need.

PROTECT YOUR SEED

Do you remember the Shunammite woman whose
seed met her need for a child? The story doesn't end there.

2 KINGS 4:18-20

18 And when the child was grown, it fell on a day, that he went out to his father to the reapers.

19 And he said unto his father, My head, my head. And he said to a lad, Carry him to his mother.

20 And when he had taken him, and brought him to his mother, he sat on her her knees till noon, and then died.

The devil attacked her for her seed. Jesus said in Mark 10:30, "You will receive a hundredfold return, but with persecution." Satan came against her blessing. That might have happened to you. You got blessed, but then the enemy came against that and attacked you, trying to take your blessing. Maybe he actually did take it from you. He took the Shunammite's blessing from her. Her son was dead on her lap. But this was not the same Shunammite woman who said to the man of God, "Don't lie to me," when he told her she would have a child. She became a different woman. She'd planted her seed, received her need, and learned some things. She wasn't going to give up her blessing.

2 KINGS 4:21-23

21 And she went up, and laid him [her son] on the bed of the man of God, and shut the door upon him, and went out.

22 And she called unto her husband, and said, Send me, I pray thee, one of the young men, and one of the asses, that I may run to the man of God, and come again.

23 And he said, Wherefore wilt thou go to him to day? it is neither new moon, nor sabbath. And she said, It shall be well.

She didn't give up her seed; she protected it. That seed had brought her a blessing, and she wasn't going to let the devil take it from her. That seed was still alive to her, because a seed doesn't quit working unless the ground says, "Stop." The ground is your heart. When your heart — your spirit — gives up, it is telling the seed to stop. But, if you won't give up — if in the middle of circumstances you will say, "My seed is out there, and it shall be well" — then it shall be well. Don't be moved by what you see or feel. Only be moved by what you believe: *It is well.*

In the rest of 2 Kings 4, we read that the Shunammite woman ran up to the mountaintop where Elisha was. He saw her coming and sent Gehazi to her to find out what was going on. Elisha told him to ask three questions: "Is it okay with your husband?" "Is it okay with you?" and "Is it okay with the child?"

Gehazi asked the Shunammite, "Is it okay with you?"

She answered, "It is well."

"Is it okay with your husband?" he asked.

She said, "It is well."

"Is it okay with the child?" (Now remember, her child is dead on the prophet's bed.)

She said, "It is well." She wasn't giving up on that seed.

Then Elisha said, "The Lord has shown me that something is going on. I don't know what it is, but this woman isn't giving up on her seed." The prophet went to the dead boy, and the Word of God says he put his nose on the boy's nose, his eyes on the boy's eyes, his cheeks on the boy's cheeks, and his hands on the boy's hands. The boy began to stir. The prophet did the same thing again — nose to nose, eyes to eyes, cheek to cheek, mouth to mouth. And the boy was raised from the dead. (2 Kings 4:18-37.)

It doesn't matter if your finances are dead or if your marriage is dead, don't give up on your seed. A seed will meet any need. It might take two years to manifest a harvest, but when it comes, it will be right on time.

GOD WILL PROVIDE

God told the Israelites when they were in the wilderness that He would supply their every need. Each day He gave them manna, but they were to eat only enough for that one day. On the sixth day, He gave them each two loaves of manna. Everyone received a double portion on the sixth day of the week, because on the seventh day they weren't to gather any food. They were only to praise the Lord and rest.

Many people today have strayed from that way of thinking, and they think they have to work two jobs in order to make it, even when those two jobs are keeping them from going to church and praising God. These people do not realize and understand that their seed will provide for their need, and instead of being in the house of God, they are pushing a dead end job.

You might be saying, "Yes, Bishop Butler, that's easy for you to say, because your job is on Sunday." Yes, it is, but I wasn't always in full-time ministry. And I always made sure that I had a job that allowed me to be in church on Sunday. That's all there is to it. I decided that I was going to be in the house of the Lord. I believe that if I serve God, He will supply my needs. He has done it in the past, He is still doing it today, and He will continue to do so, because I have a whole bunch of seed sown in faith. And I am obedient to the Lord, so I will never lack. God will do the same for you if you will trust Him to be your Provider. Take hold of these principles of seed, faith, and obedience.

REJOICE FOR THE HARVEST

What is your need? Do you need loved ones to be saved? Do you need them to be filled with the Holy Ghost? Do you need to be healed? Do you need a baby? Whatever it is, a seed will meet your need. That's why offering time at church is a time to shout — because you know what a seed will do for you. Sowing seed ought to make you glad, not sad.

The devil has lied to you long enough. Your job can't meet your needs, your spouse can't meet your needs, and all your intellect can't meet your needs. It's time to get over into the realm of the spirit, plant the seed, and watch God move on your behalf. This revelation of "a seed will meet any need" will change your life if you will let it. Seed time and harvest will work for you.

MANIFESTATIONS OF GOD'S GLORY

Some people are believing just to barely get by. However, it's not the will of God for you to barely get by. He wants you to go beyond that so there can be a manifestation of His glory in your life. God's will is that His glory be manifested in you — in your wallet, in your body, on your job, and in your family. The manifestation of His glory is supposed to fill the house.

But it's up to you, not God. His glory is waiting to manifest itself, but whether or not that happens depends on what you do. There are three things you need to do: Live a lifestyle of obedience unto God; stay in faith as you do whatever God and His Word tell you to do; and sow your best seed — with the right motive — into good ground, because a seed will meet any need!

Endnotes

Chapter 2

[1] Strong, James, *Strong's Exhaustive Concordance of the Bible,* "Hebrew and Chaldee Dictionary," "Greek Dictionary of the New Testament." Nashville: Abingdon, 1890. "Greek," p. 73, entry #5218, s.v. "hupakoe."

About the Author

Bishop Keith A. Butler is the founder and senior pastor of Word of Faith International Christian Center.

Word of Faith International Christian Center was founded on January 14, 1979, and is a congregation of 16,000 plus members and 200 employees. The main church is located on a beautiful 110-acre campus in Southfield, Michigan, where multiple services are held in the 5,000 seat auditorium. He also pastors Faith Christian Centers in Smyrna, Georgia, which began in August 1993 and in Phoenix, Arizona, which began in September 1997.

Bishop Butler is a pastor and a Bible teacher with ministerial emphasis on teaching line-by-line and applying God's Word to people's daily lives. He ministers in seminars, conventions and churches throughout the country and in third-world nations.

Bishop Butler is an author and conference speaker who travels all over the world. He and his lovely wife, Deborah, have three children who are all active in the work of the ministry: Pastor and Mrs. Keith A. Butler II, Minister MiChelle Butler and Ms. Kristina Butler.

You may contact Keith Butler
by writing:

Word of Faith Publications
P.O. Box 3247
Southfield, Michigan 48037-3247

www.wordoffaithicc.org

Please include
your prayer requests
and comments when you write

Other Books by Keith Butler

Hell: You Don't Want To Go There!
Success Strategies From Heaven
Angels, God's Servants for You
God's Plan for You
The Grace of God

Available from your local bookstore.

Harrison House
Tulsa, Oklahoma 74153

Prayer of Salvation

A born-again, committed relationship with God is the key to a victorious life. Jesus, the Son of God, laid down His life and rose again so that we could spend eternity with Him in heaven and experience His absolute best on earth. The Bible says, "For God so loved the world, that he gave his only begotten Son, that whosoever believeth in him should not perish, but have everlasting life" (John 3:16).

It is the will of God that everyone receive eternal salvation. The way to receive this salvation is to call upon the name of Jesus and confess Him as your Lord. The Bible says, "That if thou shalt confess with thy mouth the Lord Jesus, and shalt believe in thine heart that God hath raised him from the dead, thou shalt be saved. For whosoever shall call upon the name of the Lord shall be saved" (Romans 10:9,13).

Jesus has given salvation, healing, and countless benefits to all who call upon His name. These benefits can be yours if you receive Him into your heart by praying this prayer:

Heavenly Father, I come to You admitting that I am a sinner. Right now, I choose to turn away from sin, and I ask You to cleanse me of all unrighteousness. I believe that Your Son, Jesus, died on the cross to take away my sins. I also believe that He rose again from the dead so that I may be justified and made righteous through faith in Him. I call upon the name of Jesus Christ to be the Savior and Lord of my life. Jesus, I choose to follow You, and I ask that You fill me with the power of the Holy Spirit. I declare right now that I am a born-again child of God. I am free from sin, and full of the righteousness of God. I am saved in Jesus' name, Amen.

If you have prayed this prayer to receive Jesus Christ as your Savior, or if this book has changed your life, we would like to hear from you. Please write us at:

Harrison House Publishers
P.O. Box 35035
Tulsa, Oklahoma 74153

The Harrison House Vision

Proclaiming the truth and the power
Of the Gospel of Jesus Christ
With excellence;

Challenging Christians to
Live victoriously,
Grow spiritually,
Know God intimately.